Start a 501c3 Nonprofit That Doesn't Ruin Your Life

How to Legally Structure Your Nonprofit to Avoid I.R.S. Trouble, Lawsuits, Financial Scandals & More!

Attorney Audrey K. Chisholm

Start Your Tax Exempt Nonprofit, LLC

Dedication

I would like to thank God for my loving husband, Dr. Juan P. Chisholm, and our three beautiful girls and our handsome son. You all inspire me every day to keep making a difference!

Giving Back

A portion of proceeds from book sales will be donated to 501c3 charitable nonprofit organizations nationwide.

Free Gift

Schedule your FREE 30-minute Start Your Nonprofit Consultation (Value: $450) by visiting **www.StartYourTaxExemptNonprofit.com** if you are interested in having our law firm help you start your own nonprofit organization

Special Offer

Get a FREE bonus chapter by signing up for my mailing list below: http://eepurl.com/bOvTef

Contents

What are Financial Statements

Why Financial Statements Are Important

3 Types of Financial Statements

How to Create Financial Statements

Can nonprofit founders and get paid for working for a nonprofit?

Can board members get paid for working for a nonprofit?

How much can you legally pay yourself?

How to legally go about paying yourself and others?

The easiest way to calculate payroll taxes for employees

What happens if you don't follow the I.R.S. executive compensation guidelines?

How to Keep Records that Meet I.R.S. Standards

Legal Records

Asset Records

Human Resources & Vendor Records

Financial Records

Corporate Minute Book

Do you have to show people your financials or other records when asked?

Chapter One

Introduction

C an starting a 501c3 nonprofit really ruin your life? Absolutely - if you don't know what you're doing. The way you start your nonprofit matters.

It's easier than ever to file forms yourself or use do-it-yourself websites thinking you're saving a few bucks. But the mistakes and legal ramifications that can come from starting your charity without guidance - can cost you thousands to hundreds of thousands if you're not careful.

Unfortunately, I've seen good people face irreparable damage to their personal reputation and their reputation in the community, in addition to losing money as a result of costly mistakes that could have easily been avoided.

So, is the solution to not start a 501c3 nonprofit? Absolutely not.

I believe that 501c3 nonprofits are powerful vehicles that allow us to make a difference in our society and provide personal enrichment and fulfillment to founders, board members, volunteers and community stakeholders that are involved.

I know that starting my own 501c3 nonprofit positively changed my life - and I believe it can do the same for you.

I also know that the solution to having a bad experience with your nonprofit is to educate yourself and learn the common pitfalls so that you can avoid them - before you get started.

This book will help you do just that.

My goal is to share with you in plain English how to legally structure your nonprofit to avoid I.R.S. trouble, avoid getting kicked off of your board, avoid financial scandals, lawsuits and many of the other common pitfalls that no one is discussing.

Does it include everything?

Absolutely not. But it will give you a solid foundation as to many of the most common pitfalls and what you can do to avoid them.

So, sit back and let's get started.

Chapter Two

Why I Wrote This Book

My goal for writing this book is simple. I learned the importance of starting your nonprofit the right way the hard way when starting my own nonprofit. Since then, I've dedicated my professional life to educating people on how to avoid these pitfalls and start a sustainable charity that can benefit the community and society as a whole.

Here is my story.

When I was a sophomore in college at the age of 17, I felt inspired by God to do something to make a difference. I had a sincere desire to teach high school students the things that high school didn't teach me. I wanted to start a nonprofit that would host an annual leadership conference and events that would teach students how to start a business, how to graduate from college debt free, how to manage their money and how to be a leader on campus and in your community. I believed in the difference this organization would make and I decided to step out on faith and do it!

I didn't know any of the common pitfalls associated with starting such an endeavor - so I made a lot of mistakes.

1. I struggled with fundraising (primarily because I waited too

long to file our paperwork among other things) – I'll share the best time to start your nonprofit to avoid this issue.

2. I ran into issues with my board of directors (because I didn't get professional advice before structuring my board of directors. I'll share some of the key things you need to know).

3. I almost lost my nonprofit's name to 3 other organizations because I thought we already owned the name since we had registered with the state. I will share how filing paperwork with the state, setting up a website and even buying a domain name do not by themselves give you ownership of a name and let you know exactly what you need to do to legally own your nonprofit's name.

4. I missed out on grants and funding opportunities earlier on (I didn't have the right paperwork). I will share what you need to have when getting started.

5. And more!

The good news is that I dedicated years to learning the right way to start and run nonprofits. I served on the board of a large nonprofit organization for 8 years along with the former President of the New York Stock Exchange, university presidents and other professionals. I learned best practices for how successful nonprofits are run.

I also went to law school, studied nonprofit law and learned the strategies that some of the largest law firms use when forming successful nonprofits.

I then chose to start and grow my own law firm that is committed to helping 1 million people start their own 501c3 nonprofits and avoid the mistakes that I made and others have made over the years.

My law practice, Chisholm Law Firm, PLLC

(www.ChisholmFirm.com), has successfully formed 501c3 tax-exempt nonprofit organizations for clients throughout the United States ranging from startups to a Fortune 500 company. We have successfully established the following types of nonprofits: youth organizations, schools, churches, ministries, healthcare organizations, drug rehabilitation programs, animal rights organizations, homelessness prevention centers, cancer patient services, athletic services, women's issues, marriage enrichment organizations and more with a 100% success rate for 501c3 nonprofit approvals by the I.R.S. (*Disclaimer: Past results do not determine future outcomes). Our clients range from college students to professionals as well as professional athletes (NFL players, a Major League Baseball Player, a Professional Basketball Player and more!)

I also restructured my own nonprofit, Revolution Leadership®, Inc. so that we could take advantage of major funding opportunities. Since then, my nonprofit obtained 501c3 tax-exempt status and it has grown into an organization that has served almost 2,000 students and has awarded over 40 college scholarships. Revolution Leadership® has received major grants from Wells Fargo®, Enterprise® as well as corporate sponsorships from Wal-mart®, Olive Garden® and Chick-fil-A® to name a few.

While representing all of those clients and helping them start their nonprofits - I have witnessed firsthand the costly mistakes that good intentioned founders, board members, and volunteers make all of the time.

My hope is that this book will share many of the ways you can avoid costly mistakes when starting and structuring your 501c3 nonprofit.

I believe that anyone can start and grow a sustainable nonprofit if given the right information - and I would like to provide you with everything I wish I had known when I started mine.

- Audrey K. Chisholm, Esq.

Chapter Three

Chapter 1: The Basics About 501c3 Nonprofits

What Is a Nonprofit?

For me, it all started my sophomore year of college. I was 17 years old and a student at Florida State University. On this particular day, I wasn't feeling well so I went to my dorm room after class to get some rest. While I was in my bed, I felt like God vividly gave me a powerful vision of starting a nonprofit. I knew that it was supposed to help students learn the things that often aren't taught in traditional high schools, such as entrepreneurship, financial management, leadership, and self-esteem. I started writing everything down and knew that fulfilling this purpose would forever change my life as well as the lives of the students we would impact.

That is apart of my story of starting a nonprofit. What is yours?

You may be reading this book as a nonprofit founder, board member, volunteer, donor, nonprofit professor, etc. We all have a story as to how we became passionate about helping other people.

Unfortunately, our passion alone can leave us lacking critical knowledge as it relates to making decisions to legally protect ourselves and the nonprofits we care about. That is what this book is about.

We're going to start our journey together with some important definitions. Before we can learn how to avoid the pitfalls of starting a 501c3 nonprofit, we first need to know what a nonprofit is so that we're all on the same page.

A nonprofit by definition is an organization that is created to advance a particular cause - but not for the purpose of making a profit. Nonprofit organizations range from large charities and foundations to small grassroots organizations that benefit a school, church or community.

A nonprofit isn't owned by any one individual but instead is run collectively by a board of directors. Also, even though a nonprofit is allowed to sell goods and services and make a profit if there is a profit at the end of the year, the extra money does not go into the founder's pockets. Instead, it is reinvested in the nonprofit to continue to further their charitable purpose (We'll talk about how the founder of a nonprofit can legally get paid a salary later in the book but I just want to establish a framework for our discussion for now).

What Is the Difference Between a Nonprofit and a For-Profit?

Now that we have a working definition for a "nonprofit" let's compare it to a "for-profit" business. A "for profit" business is generally created to sell a good or service with the goal of making a "profit" for the owners or shareholders of the business.

When you think of a for-profit company, think of most of the goods and services that you use every day. Behind those products and services are companies that are constantly innovating with the purpose of reducing their costs, offering more products and raising their prices all with the goal of making more profit for their owners and shareholders.

For-profit businesses are owned by individuals. This means that if there is money left over at the end of the year, this money is paid out to the individuals that own the business and can be deposited into their personal bank accounts. If they ever decide to close the business, they can sell everything the business owns and then keep the proceeds for themselves after any bills and debts have been paid.

What Is a 501c3 Nonprofit?

Now that we know what a nonprofit is in general, let's talk about what a 501c3 nonprofit is and how it can benefit you. A 501c3 nonprofit is a special type of nonprofit that is governed by Section 501c3 of the Internal Revenue Code and has been approved by the I.R.S. as a charitable organization.

The most important thing for you to know is that Section 501c3 of the Internal Revenue Code shares very clear guidelines that a nonprofit must follow to be approved by the I.R.S. as a "tax-exempt" charitable organization. Once approved by the I.R.S., the nonprofit no longer has to pay state or federal taxes on any donations received.

Nonprofits that have achieved 501c3 tax-exempt status must follow a list of guidelines that are designed to make sure that the nonprofit is created for a charitable, educational, scientific or religious purpose as defined by the I.R.S. Code. We will discuss more of those rules later.

But for now, you just need to know that 501c3 nonprofits are nonprofit organizations that do not have to pay federal or state taxes on the donations they receive when they are operating in compliance with Section 501c3 of the I.R.S. Code.

Do You Qualify to Be A 501c3 Tax-exempt Nonprofit?

Now that we understand what a 501c3 nonprofit is, let's talk about how to know if the nonprofit you want to start qualifies to become one. Section 501c3 of the Internal Revenue Code is the section that lays out the criteria for nonprofits to be considered tax-exempt under this section of the Code.

In this section of the I.R.S. code, a 501c3 nonprofit is defined as a nonprofit that is "organized and operated exclusively for exempt purposes." This means that the only purpose of your organization should be a religious, educational, charitable, scientific or literary purpose.

There are other types of organizations that are tax-exempt but many of them fall under other sections of the I.R.S. code. For example, there is a different section for civic leagues or real estate title companies. Fraternal societies, as well as insurance associations, also have their own sections of the code. So, the first thing you want to do is to make sure that you fall under Section 501c3 instead of one of the other sections of the code. Diving into all of the different types of nonprofits that qualify for 501c3 status is a bit beyond the scope of this book, but you can visit the I.R.S. website (www.IRS.gov) for a complete listing of 501c3 criteria and qualifying organizations. My law firm includes this evaluation free of charge for our clients to let them know up front if their proposed nonprofit will qualify.

How to Know if You Are Already 501c3 Tax-Exempt?

Once you know that you qualify to be a 501c3, you should take a moment to make sure that your organization isn't already an approved 501c3 tax-exempt organization if your nonprofit is already operating. The easiest way to do this is to look up your nonprofit using the I.R.S. website. If you go to www.irs.gov, you can use the **Exempt Organizations Select Check** tool which will allow you to type the name of your nonprofit or the taxpayer identification number and search to see if your tax-exempt status is active with the I.R.S.

This is an important step! As I mentioned earlier, when I first started my nonprofit, I was doing a routine search only to see that my nonprofit's tax-exempt status had been revoked. I later learned that it was only because we did not file one of the required documents (which we will discuss later in the book) but I never would have known had I not taken the time to look my nonprofit up.

Here is the link:

Exempt Organizations Select Check

https://www.irs.gov/charities-non-profits/exempt-organization s-select-check

Benefits of 501c3 Nonprofits vs. Other Business Entities

Now that we understand what a 501c3 nonprofit is and are confident that your organization would qualify, let's talk about the benefits that a nonprofit receives when it applies and is approved for 501c3 tax-exempt status. Understanding this will give us context as we begin to explore the ways that you can protect yourself legally when starting a 501c3 nonprofit. But first, here are some of the benefits:

1. **Apply for Grants.** 501c3 nonprofits are often eligible to apply for federal grants, state grants, and private grants from corporations and foundations to help them fulfill their charitable purposes. A grant is money or resources that are given to an organization to carry out a specific purpose.

For example, a nonprofit that raises health awareness could receive grant funding to host a community health fair from local doctors, hospitals, pharmaceutical companies, etc.

2. **Accept Donations.** 501c3 nonprofits can accept donations from individuals and businesses to help them accomplish their mission.

For example, a nonprofit formed to educate youth on sports safety would likely attract corporate sponsorships from energy drink companies, sports apparel stores, and even athletic trainers whose donations could be used to purchase uniforms for the students, athletic gear, host, and seminars, as well as hire staff and open an office.

3. **Donations are Tax-Deductible.** Donors that give to 501c3 nonprofits can receive a tax write-off for donations they make to qualified tax-exempt nonprofits throughout the course of the year.

4. **Purchases are Tax-Free.** Qualified 501c3 tax-exempt nonprofits can buy items that help further their charitable purpose without being required to pay sales taxes on those items.

5. **Personal Liability is Limited.** Generally speaking, forming a nonprofit can protect its founder, board members and volunteers from being sued individually in lawsuits as a result of the activities of the nonprofit (some exceptions apply which we will discuss later).

The Laws that Govern 501c3 Nonprofits

Now that we understand the benefits associated with 501c3 nonprofits, let's discuss the last thing we need to know as it relates to 501c3 basics which are the laws that apply to 501c3s. Why is this important? Because we'll reference these government agencies throughout the book when we begin our discussion on how we can avoid legal pitfalls when starting a 501c3.

In essence, there are a lot of different regulatory agencies that nonprofits have to comply with. I'll give an overview of the most important ones. The key is to not feel overwhelmed. Instead, you'll want to pay careful attention to upcoming chapters where we discuss specific things you need to do (and avoid doing) to avoid liability and legal repercussions.

As long as you take care of those, and act as a reasonable person by adhering to the general principles outlined in this book – you'll put yourself in the best position to successfully avoid liability.

Federal Law and the I.R.S.

The term "federal" usually relates to things concerning all 50 states. Thus, federal laws apply to 501c3 nonprofits in each state regardless of which state you live in. On the federal level, tax-exempt nonprofits are primarily governed by the Internal Revenue Service. The I.R.S. is the division within the federal government that reviews applications for tax-exempt status and approves nonprofits that qualify. The department that oversees this process is called the Tax Exempt and Government Entities division. They manage the entire process and also oversee compliance matters.

State Law

The next body of laws that you need to be aware of relate to state law. On the state level, nonprofits must follow the laws within their state. This usually means registering their nonprofit within the state in order to operate and fundraise. They are also responsible for making sure they follow the rules as it relates to property taxes, sales taxes as well as not offending the attorney general's regulations against fraudulent activities that could harm consumers.

Local and municipal regulations

In addition to federal and state law, nonprofits need to be mindful of local and municipal regulations. These laws often relate to your local, city and county government. Nonprofits will need to apply for any occupational licenses for home offices, signage regulations for certain neighborhoods or areas, permits for events and any other requirements if required by their local government or municipality.

Sarbanes-Oxley

Next, nonprofits are also governed by legislation passed by Congress. Named after the sponsors of the bill, Sarbanes Oxley is a law designed to help regulate publicly held companies in an effort to prevent fraud. The two main parts of Sarbanes Oxley that apply to nonprofits include a requirement that you cannot retaliate or punish people that are whistleblowers because they choose to report questionable activities within your nonprofit.

Under this law, nonprofits also cannot get rid of, hide or change any evidence or documents that could hurt an investigation. Nonprofits can benefit from the guidelines included within the law that encourage organizations to have an independent audit or auditing committee. Just make sure that the firm you hire is not involved in performing other financial or recordkeeping services for the nonprofit so that you avoid any conflicts of interest.

The Pension Protection Act (PPA)

Lastly, nonprofits should be familiar with the Pension Protection Act (PPA). PPA legislation changed some of the rules relating to tax-exempt nonprofits in a way that has affected hundreds of thousands of nonprofit organizations. Under the PPA, tax-exempt organizations that have $25,000 or less in gross receipts are required to file an annual nonprofit return. If they do not do this for three years in a row, their tax-exempt status is automatically revoked.

This law is important because it means that even if you have a small nonprofit – you still need to stay on top of the annual filings or you may lose your tax-exempt status and will need to reapply. I was a victim of this change in legislation.

Before I became an attorney, this law was passed and it added an additional reporting requirement for small nonprofits. Since I did not have a nonprofit attorney that I was actively working with, I didn't know about the change until I received a letter from the I.R.S. that they had taken away my nonprofit's tax-exempt status for failure to file our annual report.

I still remembered how scared I was realizing that we had lost our tax-exempt status because of something I did not know. We then had to spend time and money filing everything all over again. Thankfully, we were approved once again, but it made me dedicated to learning everything I could about nonprofit compliance so that I could avoid that ever happening again.

Again, this list of laws to be aware of is not exhaustive. Nonprofits still have to follow civil and criminal laws as well as other statutes and ordinances which are not listed because quite frankly there are too many. My goal was just to share the most important laws - and encourage you to meet with your nonprofit attorney to make sure you are in compliance or if you want to explore all of them in more detail.

Now that we have a good overview of many of the laws that govern 501c3 tax-exempt nonprofits, let's talk about some key principles as it relates to starting a 501c3 nonprofit.

P.S. - If you've already started your 501c3, feel free to skip the next chapter!

Chapter Four

Chapter 2: Starting Your 501c3 Nonprofit

A fter getting the initial idea for starting my nonprofit, I was filled with excitement! I immediately started writing down all of my ideas and dreaming of the incredible things that the organization would be able to do to help students. I had no idea that in helping others, I would also be positively impacted by the journey ahead.

How Starting A Nonprofit Benefits You

Now that you understand an overview as to the basics regarding 501c3 nonprofits, let's talk about how starting one can benefit you personally. You may even be asking "why should I start a nonprofit when I can just donate or support an existing nonprofit?" In many instances, helping others through starting your nonprofit may benefit you in more ways than it will even benefit the people you are helping! Why am I sharing this with you? Well, it's important that you understand these personal benefits up front because they will help keep you motivated when we dive into the heavier parts of our discussion about ways to avoid the legal pitfalls.

Here are just a few ways that starting a 501c3 nonprofit can benefit you:

1. **Personal fulfillment** - Have you ever felt like you want more meaning in your life? Ever wanted to feel more significance? Or a feeling that you have a personal calling to help others or make a difference? Many of our clients have shared that they have achieved a measure of personal success and want to give back. Even if they are not independently wealthy, they feel fortunate to have overcome circumstances or to have expertise or insight in certain areas and want to help people in need or those less fortunate. They want to use their gifts and talents to make a difference in their community and beyond. Starting a nonprofit has given them a sense of meaning and fulfillment that their careers, professional associations, or even friends and family have not.

2. **Tax benefits** - Are you a high-earning individual? Are you anticipating an increase in finances from a significant raise from your job, inheritance, sale of stock, sale of real estate, business growth, equity distribution, business sale, etc.? Are you a lawyer, doctor, professional athlete, celebrity, or other high-earning individual? Many of our clients benefit from the significant tax write-offs they receive from starting their own nonprofit. Generally speaking, the **I.R.S. allows you to deduct charitable contributions up to 50% of your adjusted gross**

income (limitations apply). The financial benefits for you and/or your business as a result of reduced tax liability can be a significant benefit in many cases.

3. **Control over your philanthropy** - You may be asking, "why don't I just donate to another nonprofit" or "how is this different from contributing to a donor-advised fund?" The main answer is control. Starting your nonprofit allows you to focus on a particular issue or need that you are passionate about in the way that you feel is most effective. Many donor-advised funds or existing nonprofits already have their own causes and methods and rarely is input solicited from donors. You will also have more control over how your funds are used. As the founder of your own nonprofit, you can make sure that funds are being used efficiently in order to have a maximum impact toward your mission. Lastly, starting your own nonprofit gives you the ability to create a legacy. Your charity can continue making an impact even when you're gone. You can get your family and friends involved and continue the work you care so deeply about. Whereas other organizations or funds may decide to abandon the cause, close their doors or even shift priorities without your input or consent.

4. **Attract More Clients** - Do you currently own a business? Would you like more referrals - without increasing your marketing costs? One of the easiest ways to promote your business is by giving back

to the community. Setting up a branded nonprofit (e.g., the Chisholm Law Firm Foundation if your business is Chisholm Law Firm) is an excellent way to build relationships with community leaders that become referral sources and passionate advocates for your business. For many of our clients, they have found that when they shifted their focus to giving back to the community through their foundation, it enhanced their business's reputation and positioning in the community. This attracts potential clients who want to support companies that align with their values. Data supports this. A survey by the Edelman Trust Barometer found that 71% of consumers are more likely to trust a business that supports a cause they care about.

5. **Attract top employees** - Many talented individuals are attracted to companies that are focused on social impact and community service. By starting a nonprofit, you highlight your company's commitment to giving back which can help you attract top talent to your company.

6. **Improve employee engagement** - If you're a business owner, more and more employees are wanting fulfillment and meaning at work. It may be hard to communicate this with some jobs. But having a foundation that gives back and provides volunteer opportunities for employees can be a way to improve employee retention.

7. **Honor a loved one** - Many of our clients have found that starting a nonprofit to honor the legacy of a loved

one through offering an annual scholarship or other charitable activity was a tremendous benefit of having a nonprofit.

8. **Legal protection** - Another benefit of our clients is knowing they can continue their existing charitable efforts without fear of having set things up improperly or exposing themselves to lawsuits. They have legal protection for themselves and for their board.

9. **Accept Large Donations** - The ability to expand your passion and grow by accepting money from others is another benefit.

10. **Helps You Stay Positive** – When you start a charity that serves food to the homeless, donates clothes to people that do not have anything to wear, or raises money to find a cure for people dying of an incurable disease, it makes it much easier for you to remain positive and thankful at work or when you are managing your responsibilities as a spouse, partner, parent, sibling, aunt or uncle, mentor, etc. This is because giving back to others can help you keep things in perspective and know that there is always someone worse off than you. Instead of complaining about your hardships, you will hopefully instead choose to think of the dire situation the people you helped are in and will be thankful that your loss or disappointment could have been far worse.

11. **Offers accountability** – When you know your efforts

are working toward a greater good, it inspires you to keep going because you know people are depending on you. The success of your nonprofit or your career accomplishments may no longer simply mean buying a new car or taking an extravagant vacation. Instead, when you know that you have committed to giving away a portion of your earnings to the 501c3 nonprofit you've started, your personal success means improving a local school, building low-income housing for the needy, providing college scholarships, or any other charitable act. I'm always encouraged by book sales because I use a portion of the proceeds to support deserving charities that are making a difference. You can do the same!

12. **Gives you perspective** – When things do not work out for you, if you have been giving back to others through your 501c3 nonprofit, it should help you to not take it personally since you know from your charitable work that failure is just a part of the road to success. For example, if you've been encouraging military veterans to embrace a fresh start with new career opportunities, it should remind you that if you ever have to start over - it's not the end of the world.

13. **Helps You Handle Stress** – Helping others helps you get your mind off of life's disappointments. If you find yourself feeling depressed, try taking the focus off of you by focusing on meeting someone else's needs. You may find that you will have a better perspective since you are

reminded that there are people dealing with far more severe situations than you and that your situation may not be as bad as you thought.

14. **Attracts Good Things to Your Life** – I have found that the more generous I am with my time (mentoring, helping, and investing in others) and my money (donating to support my 501c3 nonprofit as well as other people's charities), the more I find that people unexpectedly offer to help me or invest in my endeavors without me even having to ask. Never expect the people that you help to reciprocate. Instead, just know that God will bless you in other ways by your generosity toward the less fortunate or people in need.

15. **Helps You Enjoy Your Successes** – Success can be an unending quest. We can become so consumed by it that instead of even seeing the success we currently have, we are in constant pursuit for more. There is nothing wrong with setting new goals and pursuing them. However, we just want to make sure we're balancing our ambition with thankfulness for what we already have. Spending your time focusing on the needs of others should help you see success in any accomplishment, big or small, and have a more complete appreciation for your own journey.

These are just a few of the personal benefits that come as a result of giving back through your own 501c3 nonprofit. There are so many more but for the sake of time, we are going to move forward. Now that we know some of the ways a 501c3 nonprofit can benefit you personally, let's address the myths that hold some people back from starting their nonprofit.

9 Myths About Starting Nonprofits

If there are so many benefits that come from starting a 501c3 nonprofit, why doesn't everyone do it? Here are some of the most common reasons or "myths" that keep people from starting their own nonprofit.

1. **It's too expensive.** Many people believe you have to have enough startup money to lease an office downtown, pay five people full-time salaries as staff and have a six-figure first-year operating budget to be able to start your own nonprofit. This isn't necessarily the case. You can have a six-figure startup budget - or you can simply have the funds to pay your initial costs and then work toward gradually increase the budget.

2. **You have to be independently wealthy.** Although you have the option to start a private foundation and fund it yourself from your own wealth, public charities (which are also 501c3s) are not expected to do this. Instead, a public charity is designed to be funded by donations from the general public, not your own pockets. This means you can get money from donations, grants, corporate sponsorships, etc. to run your nonprofit. You don't have to be wealthy to make a difference.

3. **You need a nonprofit degree.** Thanks to technology, managing and running a nonprofit has never been easier. There are a host of apps, websites, and online tools that are available to simplify the process of project management, donor relationship management, payroll, record keeping, bookkeeping, tracking

donations, and more. You do not need a college degree in nonprofit management to successfully start and run your own.

4. **You need lots of free time.** Many people feel that their schedules are already full with demanding jobs, family commitments, church and community involvement and caring for pets in addition to finding time to work-out, vacation, travel, enjoy hobbies, spend time with friends, etc. They may feel that spending valuable time working on their nonprofit means they may have less time to advance their own career or professional goals. The good news is that you can do all of those things while still having a successful nonprofit. We will discuss later specific strategies for managing and leveraging your time by delegating to volunteers and staff to achieve your goals for your nonprofit.

5. **You need experience running a nonprofit.** Some people feel you need actual past management experience running a nonprofit before starting your own. This is not true. You need to be willing to educate yourself and/or hire professionals that can offer guidance to supplement your inexperience - but you do not have to have had a previous career in the nonprofit industry to be successful.

6. **You need to already have a nonprofit plan.** To get started, you don't have to have anything except your idea. I have personally helped many nonprofit founders over the years start their nonprofit when all they had was their concept. If you build a good team around you, including someone experienced with nonprofit startups such as a nonprofit attorney, you can share your vision and allow them to handle the paperwork and execute your plans. (We will discuss this later in the book in the chapter about hiring a nonprofit attorney and building a team).

7. **You need to be able to live off of your savings since you can't get paid.** Nonprofits can legally pay competitive salaries, offer benefits, and retirement plans to founders that choose to work for the nonprofit. You can also hire staff and employees to help fulfill your mission. I'll share exactly how to legally pay yourself and others later in the book.

8. **You can't charge for your services.** Some people want to offer a professional service through their nonprofit (music lessons, computer coding lessons, etc.) but are discouraged thinking they would not be able to charge for them. Nonprofits can earn a profit and can charge for their services as long as they are following the rules.

9. **There are already too many nonprofits.** Some people feel that all of the "good" ideas are already taken. They feel that everything has already been created by other people and that surely their idea of a nonprofit is already being done. They fear that there is simply too much competition among the millions of nonprofits already in existence and that donors will feel even more frustrated with yet one more choice if they start their own nonprofit.

The truth is that there are a lot of nonprofits in existence. And there may, in fact, be someone else that is doing something similar to what you want to do. But none of those things in and of themselves should discourage you. Why? Because if the existing nonprofits were doing such a great job - you wouldn't see the need that you're seeing.

Here is what I mean. There are a lot of restaurants. Why are there so many? Wouldn't potential restaurateurs reference the fact that there are others in existence that already serve Italian food as a reason not to start their restaurant? No. Because they realize that even though they exist - they are not reaching everyone. The existing restaurants may reach people that want fast and cheap Italian food - but maybe not people that want an elegant sit-down experience and are willing to pay a premium for that.

Overall, there are a number of "myths" that can stop you only if you let them. Many people have overcome these same myths and have started nonprofits that have impacted others. You can do the same thing!

Now that we've addressed the "myths" that hold some people back, let's talk about what it really takes to start a 501c3 nonprofit.

What Does it Take to Start Your Own Nonprofit

If you're thinking about starting your own 501c3 nonprofit, there are several things that you should consider before deciding to move forward - but they may not be what you think they are.

Over the years, I've had the pleasure of advising clients throughout the United States about making the decision to start their own 501c3. Here are just a few things that I've found helpful that may assist you in understanding what you need to start your own 501c3 nonprofit:

3 Things You Need to Start Your Own Nonprofit

Passion. Starting a 501c3 nonprofit will require effort so it will certainly help if you're doing something you're passionate about. Being passionate about something just means that it relates to a core value of yours to the point where you'll be motivated to keep going because it is something that you care deeply about.

Personally, I am very passionate about helping students achieve their goals. I was a very motivated student, yet without the financial support from scholarships, I would not have been able to afford my dream of attending college. Since I am passionate about helping students, it is not work for me to grow my nonprofit because I love being able to help young people reach their goals.

If you start a nonprofit that you are passionate about - you're more likely to enjoy it more than if you were starting something that you weren't passionate about!

Commitment. You need to be willing to make a decision and stick with it! Despite how passionate you are, starting your 501c3 nonprofit will still require effort. Making a commitment to see it through will allow you to keep going even if you encounter setbacks or obstacles along the way.

When I started my nonprofit, I had a difficult time recruiting students to attend our leadership conference. It appeared that I was competing with too many options that seemed like more fun to the students that I was targeting. It felt very easy to quit because I initially was not seeing the results that I wanted.

However, I had made a commitment to starting and growing Revolution Leadership. Instead of quitting when things became tough - I used it as motivation to increase my effort and it paid off big!

Again, you want to be able to make a decision to start your 501c3 nonprofit and then commit to seeing it through even when things get tough.

Team. The last thing you need is a team. You may be wondering why I did not mention money, education, a nonprofit plan or even time. I intentionally excluded those things because if you have a solid team on board, you can manage without the others.

For example, at minimum, you'll need someone on your team that has answers to the things that you do not know. For some people, it could be finding a mentor, nonprofit manager or colleague that can assist. The downside to an informal arrangement such as that is that the person has a limited commitment to you so they may only be willing to speak with you once a month or only on weekends. They may have limited availability and are only willing to share bits and pieces of what you need to know. They also likely will not be willing to be held responsible if you rely on their advice and something goes wrong since they were doing it for free.

Instead, consider working with a professional that will make a commitment toward ensuring your success. Since you have hired them, they should have a schedule as to times that you will meet as well as a roadmap of the things that need to be done. Find someone that has worked with other people before with success. They should also have actual business systems so that they can stay on top of all of the things that need to be done. Lastly, they need to have the legal knowledge and expertise necessary to do everything the right way for you.

My law firm does just this for clients every day. Our clients are professionals that hire us because they know they want to start a 501c3 nonprofit but do not know about the process and don't have the time or desire to learn. Many of the clients of my firm do not have a business plan, have never worked for nor run a nonprofit and have more questions than answers about the process. They are hiring us as experts to handle all of the details and ensure that everything is done the right way. We do just that.

We answer all of their questions, handle all of the legal paperwork and structuring of their nonprofit as well as advise them on how to raise money, recruit volunteers, hire staff, apply for grants and grow. It is within your reach to have the same type of team working on your behalf to get things started the right way if you don't have the answers yourself. All you have to do is ask. My firm's contact information is in the resource section of the book if we can ever be of assistance.

Now that you understand what it takes to start a nonprofit, let's talk about some ideas for how you can get started small while still growing to have big results.

10 Nonprofit Ideas for Starting Small

At this point, we've talked about what you need to start a nonprofit. Now, we're going to go over a few simple ideas for starting your nonprofit small. Over the years, some of my clients have been discouraged from getting started because they felt that they needed a half million dollar annual operating budget to even consider starting their 501c3 nonprofit and making a difference. Although that works fine, it is not necessary.

It is perfectly acceptable to start small - but it doesn't mean you have to stay small (unless you want to of course). Even if your overall goal is to build schools, operate internationally, have multiple locations and a multi-million dollar budget to fund significant research - you can still get started right where you are and grow from there. Here are just a few ideas for ways that your nonprofit can start small but still make a difference:

1. **Host a Lecture Series** – You can sign up as a volunteer at a nearby school, library, university, church, community center or large corporation. Offer to share your story and resources to benefit their audience and to inspire them to make positive decisions. Remember, you only have to be one step ahead of a person to encourage or help them.

2. **Volunteer** – Think of a cause that you are passionate about (e.g., feeding the homeless, mentoring children, supporting cancer research, helping students afford a college education, etc.) Find existing charities online that focus on the areas that you care about. Contact them and ask if your 501c3 nonprofit can partner with them by volunteering at their upcoming events or projects.

Remember to follow-up if you do not hear back from them within a reasonable time. Many nonprofits are run by volunteers and have minimal paid staff. You may need you to call back if you do not get a response after your first inquiry. Do not take their lack of responsiveness personally but allow your passion to fuel your commitment by following up.

3. **Be a Mentor** – You don't have to be a celebrity to be a role model or hero to a child. There are students in need of after-school mentors that will encourage them to stay in school, make good decisions, and stay committed to their dreams. Your 501c3 nonprofit can contact local schools and community centers to find out how you can get involved. You can then recruit other volunteers to be mentors on behalf of your nonprofit as well.

4. **Donate Money** – You can agree to give a portion of your salary or income to your 501c3 nonprofit to benefit a cause you are passionate about. I personally believe in tithing (giving 10% to a church that makes a difference in the community) as well as giving

to local nonprofits. This is something I've done for years.

You can also encourage people you care about to get involved by sharing the charitable work your nonprofit is doing with your friends and family and encouraging them to join you. This can multiply the impact that you are making in the community.

For example, giving back is so important to me that I've found ways for my entire staff to participate as well. As a firm, we donate to various charities throughout the year.

Sometimes we share our charitable efforts with clients and supporters to encourage them to join in. Oftentimes we give and never even tell other people about it but we feel good knowing that we are making a difference. We also sponsor a charity each year and we volunteer throughout the year as a team. This is just one example of how you can encourage your family, friends and even co-workers to join you in a philanthropic endeavor.

5. **Donate In-Kind Goods** - Your 501c3 nonprofit can collect and donate food, clothes, toys, hygiene items, etc. to a local children's hospital to brighten a child's day, a nursing home, a homeless shelter or provide them to military troops overseas. Instead of selling your used clothes, etc., you can choose to give away your old clothing each time you purchase something new to someone else in need. You can also sell items you're not using and use the proceeds from the sales toward supporting your 501c3 charity.

6. **Offer Services** – You can contact a school, church, community center, hospital, nursing home, hospice, retirement community, and volunteer to offer professional services for free during the holidays through your 501c3.

7. **Be a Resource** - Share information you have learned with

others that are trying to get where you are. You will find that it will come back to you and you will go farther than if you kept all of your information to yourself. Brand the training, webinar, ebook, etc. that you offer under the name of your 501c3 nonprofit.

8. **Start a Campaign** – My husband and I decided early in our marriage that we wanted to start a charitable tradition for our family. We collected clothing and purchased new toys and books and launched our annual "Clothing & Toy Drive for the Homeless." Each year, donate items to a local charity or homeless shelter around the holidays to make a difference. Again, you don't have to be a billionaire to mobilize your family and even friends to do something to make a difference through your own 501c3 nonprofit.

9. **Involve Your Family** – consider taking the time to build a relationship with your family (parents, siblings, spouse, and children) and ask them to get involved with your 501c3 nonprofit. Ask them questions. Listen to their interests. Then offer ways that are meaningful to them that they can volunteer and get involved. Speak kind and encouraging words to them and inspire them to reach their goals as you collectively give back to help others.

10. **Encouraging Others** — Once you are giving back to others through your 501c3 nonprofit, be sure to encourage those around you to do the same. When you inspire others to give back, it increases the impact you are making. For example, if you begin collecting canned food to donate to a local Homeless Shelter to feed people in need, you may be successful at providing food for a few families. However, if you post a video on social media sharing with your followers online that you are committed to supporting the local Homeless Shelter in your area and encouraging them to

also donate, you are now impacting hundreds if not thousands of families.

Share openly with your supporters the causes that you believe in and the things you value. This will allow them to connect with you not only as an individual but to know that by supporting you, they are supporting something greater that will have a lasting impact on society and the world. You will find that you will attract people that will enthusiastically support your efforts because they believe in the difference you are making.

If everyone used their gifts and talents to encourage one other person to make a difference, the world would be a better place. By investing in this book, you have done just that because a portion of all proceeds are being donated to 501c3 charitable nonprofit organizations. So thank you for helping me make a difference!

Should You Incorporate your Nonprofit?

After hearing all of the great ways that you can start small with giving back through your 501c3 nonprofit, you may be thinking "Do I even need a 501c3 nonprofit?" Can't I just volunteer or donate my resources and services? Isn't it easier to just avoid all of the headache and legal paperwork?"

The answer is yes you can give back without starting a 501c3 nonprofit. However, despite the fact that you can give back without starting a 501c3 nonprofit - in most cases I still encourage you to at least consider doing so. Here is why.

Let's begin with some basic definitions. Incorporating a nonprofit is the process of filing the appropriate paperwork with your state to formally create your nonprofit as its own legal entity.

Incorporating allows your nonprofit to legally be seen as an entity that is separate from you. This is a good thing because it means in most instances that the nonprofit will be responsible for its own actions.

I understand that the formalities involved in formally incorporating your nonprofit may be a bit intimidating. Yet, they exist for a reason.

The purpose of formally registering the nonprofit with your state as an official organization is to protect you from being sued personally despite doing good deeds to help others.

For example, let's say you and the other board members of your nonprofit decide to recruit volunteers to help you build a house for the homeless. A local store donates the supplies and you divide up the tasks. In the process, one of the volunteers injures themselves on the job site. If the volunteer decides they want to sue and your nonprofit was properly incorporated and following many of the recommendations in this book, the volunteer would most likely only be able to win in a lawsuit against the nonprofit itself. This means that they would only be able to go after the money in the nonprofit's bank account to satisfy the judgment instead of being able to attach a claim to your personal checking and savings account.

Another way to say it is if you are running a nonprofit and have not formally set up the nonprofit by incorporating within your state, you are running an "unincorporated association." Even though you may feel you have saved time and money by not filing any paperwork, the risk that you assume is that you are exposing yourself to liability. This means that if anything adverse happens while you are running the nonprofit, the person or business that was injured could sue you personally. Being sued personally means that your personal bank account, property, and assets are in jeopardy and could be used to satisfy the judgment against you.

Let me share one more illustration to make this point:

Example: Ashton cared deeply about helping homeless people and wanted to do something to make a difference. He had heard from a friend that he should speak to a nonprofit attorney to set up his nonprofit the right way, but he figured the money he would spend on that would be better served going directly to the homeless.

He decided to host a pool party at his apartment complex as a fundraising event. He invited his friends, told them what he wanted to do to help the homeless and asked them to give to his vision. For dessert, Ashton sold homemade cupcakes that he baked himself. He shared with everyone that the proceeds from the cupcakes would go directly toward helping the homeless. Unfortunately, one of his guests started choking on the cupcake due to a severe nut allergy and died before reaching the emergency room.

Ashton was shocked when he was served legal papers suing him personally for the death of his guest that had choked and died on a cupcake. His lawyer shared that if the civil suit against him won, he could lose his savings and his wages could be garnished to pay the judgment.

If he had at least incorporated his nonprofit with the State, the nonprofit itself as the host of the event would have been liable instead of Ashton as an individual.

This is the reason I strongly encourage you to consider incorporating your nonprofit if you plan on doing charitable work as illustrated above. If you have a nonprofit that is incorporated, it can protect you and other individuals involved with the charity from liability as long as you did not act intentionally and were not grossly negligent. The price you pay to set it up the right way is small when compared with what it could save you if you found yourself facing a lawsuit.

How Long Does it Take to Start Your Nonprofit?

Now that you understand why it may benefit you to incorporate your nonprofit, let's talk about the time frame you can expect. Often the first question clients ask me as it relates to starting their nonprofit is "how long will the process take?" The answer to this question is "it depends."

Generally speaking, there are typically two parts to the process of starting a nonprofit. The first part is that you need to legally form or "incorporate" your nonprofit so that you can begin operating on the state level. The second part of the process includes filing the paperwork necessary for your nonprofit to become "501c3 tax-exempt" on the federal level.

Let's discuss the "incorporation" part first. As we discussed earlier, incorporating your nonprofit means filing paperwork with your state as well as with the I.R.S. to create the nonprofit as a legal entity. Once your nonprofit is incorporated, it is officially registered and able to begin operating. The timeline for this part of the process depends on how long it takes to prepare your paperwork as well as how long it takes for your state's division of corporations to approve all of the documents.

At my law firm, we don't view incorporation as a fill-in-the-blank exercise as many modern companies do. We help clients start sustainable nonprofits that are structured for growth and success in an evolving economy. As such, when my firm first meets with a client that needs to incorporate their nonprofit, we start by taking the time to learn their overall vision, short-term, and long-term goals. This is important because incorporation is about creating the legal structure of an organization and the wrong structure can lessen your chances of accomplishing your goals.

For example, some of the initial considerations when incorporating include:

1. Choosing the name of the nonprofit - We will discuss this later in the book and I will share how to avoid liability when selecting a name;

2. Selecting Board Members;

3. Selecting Nonprofit Officers - they are different from board members;

4. Nonprofit Purpose - this must be specific enough to meet the strict I.R.S. requirements but broad enough to encompass the founder's vision;

5. Asset Protection Clauses - this language helps to reduce liability on the part of the board members for actions of the nonprofit as we discussed earlier;

6. Disposition of assets - you must outline specifically how assets will be disposed of in the event that you decided to shut down the nonprofit;

7. Prohibited activities - this section should spell out activities that your nonprofit will not engage in and should be written in conformity with I.R.S. guidelines;

8. And more!

This list is not intended to be comprehensive. Instead, I

just want to give you an idea of the things that you need to consider when initially structuring your nonprofit. Instead of seeing incorporation as just being a cookie-cutter one-size-fits-all setup, see it as the actual foundation of your organization. At my firm, I've trained our entire team to focus on structuring the nonprofit the right way from the very beginning. This saves our clients both time and money because their paperwork will not need to be changed again before applying with the I.R.S. or before soliciting funding.

The second part of starting a nonprofit is applying for tax-exempt status with the I.R.S. This is the part of the process that involves completing the federal application for tax-exempt status with the I.R.S. as well as in some cases the state application for tax exemption.

How Long Does it Take to File For Tax-Exempt Status

The second part of the process can be daunting and the amount of time it will take if you are attempting to file it yourself will depend on:

• Which form(s) you're filing (some organizations qualify for the expedited review process while others require the long review process);

• How fast you are able to research the state and federal laws to make sure you're in compliance;

• The time it takes to prepare all of the ancillary documents, addendum, budget, etc. that are required based on your form;

The good news is that you do not have to figure all of this out on your own. There are firms like mine that offer a turnkey package that takes care of the entire nonprofit formation process from start to finish for our clients. We like to give ourselves at least two weeks to get the paperwork together for our clients. Once we have filed everything, it can take the I.R.S. between 2 months to 12 months to render their determination.

How to Find Time to Start Your Nonprofit?

There are people with the same 24 hours a day that you have that find time to start their nonprofits while juggling work, relationships, children and more.

What is their secret? For many of them, they hire people.

They don't spend hours on Google trying to become experts in the I.R.S. code and tax-exempt law.

They realize that the money they spend paying an expert will save them time and money.

How do they save time? Hiring an expert lets you focus on your other responsibilities instead of trying to do everything yourself. If you mess something up, you can get yourself into serious trouble with the I.R.S. You also save time by hiring an expert because you don't have to waste time continually reapplying over and over again because your application was rejected.

How does hiring someone save them money? If you try and start your nonprofit yourself - you could spend hundreds of hours trying to learn and understand the I.R.S. Code and nonprofit law. If you make $20/hour and spend 300 hours researching - which is not uncommon - you have lost $6,000. That is the same $6,000 that you could have spent hiring a professional - an expert - to do the process for you.

Hiring someone also saves you money because you can avoid costly mistakes. For example, if you apply yourself or hire a cheap company and your application is rejected - you lose the $275-$600 filing fee to the I.R.S. since it is non-refundable.

We have one client that hired three different people that were unsuccessful before hiring us. Although we were able to get her nonprofit approved - she could have saved a lot of money by hiring us the first time.

When Should You Start Your Nonprofit?

Now that you have a general understanding as to what it takes to form your nonprofit, you're probably wondering "how soon should I get started?" My law firm has a wide array of clients ranging from college students to executives, startup companies, community organizers, professional athletes to Fortune 500 companies. Yet, the answer is typically the same for everyone.

Now. The best time to get started is now.

Oftentimes, people that I speak to that are considering starting a nonprofit think that the best time to get started is once they have everything figured out. They feel that they need a professionally written business plan, board directors, a name, built their website, have a six-figure budget as a result of their fundraising, etc. Now all of those things are great - but they certainly are not necessary for us to get started.

The reason we do not encourage folks to wait until they have everything figured out is because:

1. **Guidance** - they will miss out on the value of having

a nonprofit lawyer share best practices, answer questions and provide guidance that only a trusted advisor that has worked with countless nonprofits can offer.

We've had clients hire my firm that had spent hours working on things for their nonprofit only for us to glance at it and inform them that they did not need it, they did it wrong or share with them our process for it which they enthusiastically wanted to swap for theirs.

2. **Grants & Funding** - Not everyone wants to seek outside funding for their nonprofit but if you do, grants will want to see your history with your nonprofit. This means that getting started now begins to build your history with the organization which is usually judged favorably over a nonprofit that is brand new and unproven. Which would you rather donate to? A brand new organization versus one that was at least already incorporated?

3. **I.R.S. Compliance** - The I.R.S. has different filing requirements based on how long it took you after incorporating to apply for tax-exempt status. Their rules favor organizations that filed early after starting the nonprofit.

4. **Liability Protection** - Forming your nonprofit is an investment that pays for itself due to the protection from liability. Of all the clients I have represented, none of them ever expected to be sued. Knowing that your personal life savings are not at risk makes it more than a worthy investment.

5. **Professional Image** - the professional image that forming your nonprofit gives your charity is a powerful incentive. Donors, vendors, volunteers, etc. tend to be more favorable toward organizations that have structured themselves the right way instead of organizations that have not.

However, worst case scenario, I certainly recommend forming your nonprofit no later than when you begin accepting money. Meaning, if you are asking for donations or raising money through events, then you want to make sure you are protected from liability.

Should You Have Multiple Nonprofits Within An Umbrella Nonprofit?

Lastly, let's end this chapter on starting your nonprofit with a frequently asked question. Have you ever heard the adage "Don't put all of your eggs in one basket?" Well, the same holds true in the nonprofit sector. You will want to set up different nonprofits for each nonprofit organization as soon as you can afford to do so.

Why? Because if all of your nonprofits are under the same organization, then someone that wants to sue you based on one aspect of your nonprofit (e.g., food pantry) will have access to your assets from the other nonprofit organizations (e.g., mentoring and tutoring, etc.) if they are all under the same nonprofit. As convenient as it may seem to have one "umbrella" nonprofit, major foundations and industry professionals almost always form separate entities to minimize the chances of someone being able to sue them and taking everything.

In Chapter One we learned about the Basics of Nonprofits. In Chapter Two, we learned some more general concepts about Starting a Nonprofit. Now that we have established a foundation, it is time to get to the "good stuff" and talk about how we can structure our nonprofits so that they do not ruin our life. The next chapter will kick-off that discussion by sharing "How to Avoid a Lawsuit When Choosing a Name for your Nonprofit."

Chapter Five

Chapter 3: How to Avoid a Lawsuit When Choosing a Name for your Nonprofit

*T*he name "Revolution Leadership" came to me at the same time that I was inspired to start the nonprofit. I was fortunate that the name was available despite the fact that I did not know the principles in this chapter. As a practicing attorney, I regularly encounter well-intentioned nonprofit founders that are facing legal ramifications due to them not knowing the things we are about to cover in this chapter when they initially chose their nonprofit's name.

The Importance of Your Name

In the nonprofit industry, the name you choose is very important. Your name is what donors, volunteers, board members, community leaders, corporate sponsors, etc. need to be able to remember in order to donate to you and support you. If your name is not catchy enough, or memorable enough, supporters will have a tough time spelling it. Since more and more people look up information on their phones and tablets, if it takes them too long to find you online, they may spend their time locating one of your competitors and supporting their nonprofit instead. Therefore, your goal should be to choose a name that your supporters will remember but also a name that you can legally protect.

How are Names Legally Protected?

Before we can talk about how to avoid breaking the law when it comes to choosing the name of your nonprofit, let's first understand how names are legally protected.

The body of law that governs ownership of names, logos and slogans is called trademark law. Trademark law is governed by state and federal law.

By definition, a trademark is a name (words) or a design (logo) intended to distinguish a good or service (your nonprofit) from similar goods or services by others in the market (your competition).

As long as you are using the name of your nonprofit in connection with your nonprofit services in commerce, you may be able to protect your name if certain criteria are met that we will cover in this book.

Why Do You Need a Name You Can Legally Protect?

Now that you understand how names are protected using trademarks, we need to discuss why it is important for you to choose a name for your nonprofit that you can legally protect. The reason it is important is that you will be investing hundreds and often thousands of dollars in building your brand around your nonprofit's name (e.g. buying a website, logo, merchandise, social media, marketing, etc.). Since you will be investing so much money and time, you want to choose a name that will have maximum legal protection to prevent other people from copying your nonprofit's name and using your good reputation to make a profit.

Your name also needs to be a name you can protect and own legally so that someone else does not sue you for using their name and good reputation.

The law provides that you cannot use a name that is similar to someone else's trademark to the point where it may confuse the public and make the public think that you are your competitor. This is called "trademark infringement."

Thus, the entire goal of choosing a name for your nonprofit should not only be to find something you like - but to find a name that is available and does not infringe on someone else's trademark.

Example: Ashton wanted to start a nonprofit called "Change Foundation, Inc." He shared his vision with a nonprofit attorney and hired her firm to set everything up. His attorney recommended that he let them do a legal search for the name and apply for a trademark to own the name before forming the nonprofit to make sure there were no issues with the name. Ashton refused.

After a few weeks, his nonprofit was registered. He hosted a small dinner at his home with close friends and family. He shared his vision and asked them to donate. That night, he raised $20,000 - not including the $5,000 he donated to the nonprofit to cover the costs of the event.

With his newly registered nonprofit, he hired a marketing firm to design a logo, build a custom website, create social media accounts, and make a few high-quality promotional videos sharing the story of his charity. He then hired a digital marketing company to run a series of social media ads featuring the videos and asking for donations.

Within a few weeks, the Change Foundation had thousands of new followers on social media, their promotional video went viral and he had raised an additional $100,000 from the online ad campaign.

That's when Ashton checked his mail and received a letter from an attorney in New York. The letter demanded that he immediately transfer ownership (usernames and passwords) to his social media accounts (Facebook, YouTube, Twitter) transfer ownership of his website domain name, destroy merchandise in his online store and immediately stop offering services or engaging in any other activity with the name Change Foundation. The demand letter stated that a nonprofit organization in New York had already registered a federal trademark and owned the name.

Ashton had to give up everything he had worked for, lost the $25,000 that he had invested in building his brand plus the social media followers, donors and volunteers that were connected to the old nonprofit name. He then had to spend the money all over again and rebuild for something that could have been avoided up front by having his attorney do the name search and apply for a trademark to own the name before he started using it.

How to Know if You Have a Name You Can Legally Protect?

Now that we know what our goal should be when it comes to choosing a name for our nonprofit, let's talk about the guidelines that we should take into consideration when choosing a name:

1. You cannot trademark a generic term or something that is commonly used. The United States Patent & Trademark Office (USPTO) will not let you be the only person that can own the rights to a generic term. Therefore, we want the name of our nonprofit to be unique and original (think "Google") instead of just a commonly used word or phrase.

2. The name must be used to be protected. If you stop using it and it does not appear that you will start using it again, it may be considered "abandoned." This means that someone else could technically get the name and assume ownership of it if you are no longer using it. So this is an incentive to not only start your nonprofit but to keep it going!

3. You must use the name in commerce to have rights in the name. You do not receive trademark rights just for coming up with the name. This means thinking of a great name is not enough. You'll need to put it to work in order for it to be something you can own via a registered trademark.

4. Use in commerce generally means selling or transporting the goods or displaying the services (for your nonprofit) between states or overseas. You'll need to use the name with people outside of your state to show that it merits a federal trademark. Thankfully, the internet, websites, and technology, in general, have made this requirement much easier to comply with.

5. You can reserve a name that you have not used, but you still must use it within a certain amount of time to keep your rights. My law firm has done this successfully for clients that knew they wanted to own the name but weren't quite ready to begin operations.

6. The earlier you start using the name, the better. The law rewards the first user of the mark. The sooner you start using your mark, and preferably register your mark with the federal government, the better.

7. You will only get rights to the mark in the classes (categories of goods and services) that the USPTO deems you are most likely to use or offer to the public. For example, just because you develop rights to your name in association with nonprofit services, does not mean your ownership will extend to pharmaceutical products. Someone else may be able to claim rights to the same name in that particular class if they are using the name in connection with goods or services (e.g., selling pharmaceutical products). You can apply for a trademark in multiple classes (many nonprofits own a number of trademarks) for additional fees, but will still have to prove that you actually use your mark within those categories of goods and services.

How to Know if Your Name is Too Similar?

Now that we know the general principles to consider when thinking of nonprofit names, how can you know if the name you have in mind is too similar to one that is already registered? Courts will consider several factors to decide if the name you have chosen for your nonprofit is too similar to someone else's name:

1. How similar are the names/marks?

2. How related are their products or services?

3. How strong is your mark itself?

4. In what ways will you market the goods or services associated with your mark?

5. How careful are potential buyers when selecting your goods or services?

6. What was the intent of the infringing person when they chose the mark?

7. Is there evidence that consumers are actually confused between the brands?

8. What is the probability that the companies will expand their offerings to be more similar to the other company's offerings in the future?

6 Things to Consider When Choosing a Name

Now that you know the legal standard that will be considered if a court ever has to decide if your mark is too similar to someone else's, you can keep them in mind as you are narrowing down your choices. Here are just a few more factors to consider when choosing a name for your nonprofit:

1. Easy to spell. Make sure people will not have trouble spelling your name.

2. Easy to say. Make sure the name is not difficult to pronounce. This will make people less inclined to talk about your nonprofit since they may be embarrassed about not knowing how to say the name.

3. Relevant. It is helpful if your name actually lets people know that your nonprofit is related to the nonprofit industry instead of a name that makes them think you are in another type of business.

4. Unique. The law gives the strongest legal protection to original words that you create yourself (e.g., Twitter, Google, etc.) It is far easier to claim 100% ownership rights to a name that did not exist before you ever used it. You may not want to use your last name because last names are not typically considered strong marks.

5. Ask for Feedback. Feel free to ask close friends or mentors to choose between your top options. However, you may want to consider having them sign a confidentiality or Non-Disclosure Agreement (NDA) to make sure they do not register and use your name before you do.

6. Available. Conduct an extensive legal name search to make sure that the name is available.

What is a Name Search?

Now that you feel you have chosen a good name, here is how you check to verify if it is available. The only way to know if someone already has the rights to the name that you want to use is to conduct a professional name search. This involves looking in the most common places where a person could be using the name in order to know if someone already has rights to the name. Here are the places you need to look:

1. Search for the name online. Type the name in quotation marks: "Start Your nonprofit" to see if any nonprofits in the same class (offering similar products and services) are using the name or a name very close to yours.

2. Search Federal Trademark Filings. Search for the name within the United States Patent & Trademark registrations. Visit www.USPTO.gov. You want to look at pending, active, and inactive filings as well.

3. Search State Trademark Registrations. All 50 states allow owners to register their trademark on a state level. It is often cheaper than the federal registration process and provides protection throughout the state – although a federal registration gives you rights throughout all 50 states and can supersede a state registration. You can complete this search by going to the Division of Corporations website for each state and searching their trademark filings for the name you are interested in.

4. Search state company registrations. All 50 states allow nonprofits to register their companies. You want to search to see if any other companies are registered using your name. Although registering by itself does not give them rights, using the name with their products and services to the public in commerce does. You can complete this search by going to the Division of Corporations website for each state and searching their corporate filings (be sure to look for all of the business types including nonprofits, corporations, etc.) for the name you are interested in.

5. Search domain names. You can visit www.GoDaddy.com and select the "Who Is" option to see who owns the domain name if it is already taken. Try and search for the company and owner to see if they are actively using the name in association with similar goods and services as yours.

6. Get a Legal Opinion. It's always less expensive to do things yourself. However, trademark law is interpreted very specifically. This means that just because you feel that your name is not similar, or you feel that someone has abandoned their rights to a name, does not mean the law or a judge would see it the same way. The few hundred dollars that you invest in hiring an attorney to know for sure could save you thousands of dollars defending a lawsuit later down the road.

Comprehensive Professional Name Search

My law firm offers a **Comprehensive Professional Name Search** to our clients. Our name search examines all of the sources we identified above including federal trademark filings, state trademark filings, company filings, domain names, as well as nonprofit registries and common law listings. We also include a legal opinion where we list the sources we searched, review the findings and provide you with a legal opinion on the name to let you know if we feel that it is legally protectable based on the law. The purpose of this service is to make sure our clients are not using a name that they will be sued for later.

In this chapter, we've talked about how to choose a name that can be protected legally and how to verify that it is available through having a name search done. Now, let's talk about how to protect your name from counterfeits and identity theft.

Chapter Six

Chapter 4: How to Protect Your Nonprofit's Name from Counterfeits and Identity Theft

I *still remember the awful feeling I had when I first became aware that someone was using my nonprofit's name without our permission. I remember thinking "What type of person would do this to a nonprofit that is helping students?" I was devastated and concerned at the same time. I was devastated because I knew that this was now a legal matter and I did not know how much it would cost to fix it or how long it would take.*

I was concerned because I realized that if I didn't know that I needed a trademark to own my nonprofit's name despite already being registered with the state and the I.R.S. - how many other people were in the same situation? I was a new attorney and had only been practicing law for a year. But I was so determined to make sure my nonprofit was protected that I started studying major brands such as Oprah Winfrey's media empire, NIKE, etc. to find out how they protected their intellectual property. I didn't know this at the time but the adversity I encountered motivated me to not only protect my nonprofit but to do the same for others nationwide.

Now that we've learned how to choose names that we can legally protect and make sure that they're available with name searches, let's talk about how to protect your nonprofit's name from counterfeits and identity theft. Here are three things you can do:

1. Register a federal trademark - The most important thing you can do to discourage others from imitating your nonprofit is to become the legal owner of the name through obtaining a federal trademark. We'll talk extensively about how to do this in this chapter.

2. Use the ® sign - As a registered trademark owner, you will legally be able to use the circle-R when you refer to your nonprofit to put others on notice that you are the legal trademark owner. For example, when I refer to Revolution Leadership® I use the circle-R at the end to let others know that the brand is legally owned and protected.

3. Monitor your brand - Once you have registered your nonprofit's name, you will want to sign up with a service to monitor the use of the name. There are companies that will monitor trademark filings for you as well as online activity to let you know if anyone else is trying to infringe on your ownership rights. You can also sign up for free Google alerts which will let you know if someone is using your charity's name on the internet. Just search for the words "google alerts" online to sign up.

Now that we know some practical ways to protect your nonprofit's name from counterfeits and identity theft, let's talk specifically about when you need a trademark and how to get one.

Do you Need A Trademark If You Have Incorporated Your Nonprofit?

Some people think that just because they incorporated or formed their nonprofit with their State that they do not need to apply for a federal trademark to own the name. Please know that registering your nonprofit with your state by filing Articles of Incorporation *does not* give you legal ownership of the name. Someone else in another state could have registered the exact same name and may have been using the name longer than you have – which would mean they have already acquired ownership rights to the name you are using.

Do you Need A Trademark If You Have A Fictitious Name or D/B/A?

Filing and receiving a fictitious name or "doing business as" (D/B/A) within your state also does not give you ownership rights to a name. Some people choose to avoid the investment involved with filing for a federal trademark by filing for a "fictitious name" instead. Again, a fictitious name does not give you ownership or legal rights to the name in and of itself. If someone else was using the name before you or had already registered a federal trademark, they would most likely have superior rights to the name.

Should You Get a State Trademark or Federal Trademark?

Lastly, instead of paying for a federal trademark, some people apply for a state trademark thinking it will give them the same legal protection. Once again, this is not true. A federal trademark has more weight than a state trademark.

If you register the name of your nonprofit for a state trademark and someone else registers the same name with the federal government for a federal trademark, their rights would likely be superior to yours. Meaning, they would likely be able to keep the name and you would have to use a different one and possibly be liable to them for damages.

Benefits of a Federal Trademark

On the other hand, there are a number of benefits to having a federal trademark to own the name of your nonprofit. Some of the benefits include:

1. Ownership. The first benefit of having a federal trademark is the peace of mind that comes from knowing that you have legal ownership to the mark. This means that if another nonprofit in another city, county, or state desires to use your mark, they have to get your permission (unless their use falls within "Fair Use" which is also discussed in this book). This prevents you from spending money buying a domain name, building a website, having a graphic designer create a logo, establishing social media profiles with a name, only to have to spend all of the money all over again because you had to take it down since someone else already owned the name.

2. Make Money through Licensing. Another benefit of owning a federal trademark is that it provides another stream of income for your nonprofit. Meaning, once you have established a brand, you could license, or give other people the right, to use your mark on other products in exchange for paying you a royalty.

Example: Christina starts a socially conscious nonprofit that builds a substantial following of young adults. Since all of her social media followers are familiar with the name of Christina's nonprofit, and they associate the name with a culture that supports social causes, she has her attorney draft an agreement with an organic t-shirt company. The organic t-shirt company wants to reach more customers that will be willing to pay a premium for their shirts in exchange for knowing that the t-shirts will not harm the environment. They agreed to pay Christina a royalty of 5% for every t-shirt they sell that features her nonprofit's logo. This becomes an additional stream of income, or source of revenue, for Christina that she does not have to work for. As her nonprofit's popularity increases, she strikes similar deals with companies that sell organic coffee mugs, novelty items, work-out clothes, and even a perfume line.

3. Get Paid When People Wrongfully Use Your Mark. Owning a federal trademark also means that you have the right to sue someone in federal court for money damages if they use your mark without your permission.

Example: Stacy finds out that there is a nonprofit in Indiana that has the same name as her nonprofit. They have started using the logo of the nonprofit Stacy founded (despite the fact that she has a registered federal trademark for the logo) without her permission.

The fraudulent organization starts gaining popularity. Stacy contacts her lawyer and has them send a legal notice to the company demanding that they immediately stop using her legally protected logo. She checks their website frequently and sees that they have not changed the logo or name after having received the notice.

She then hires her lawyer to file a lawsuit against the company in federal court. She requests that the judge not only award her the profits that the company has illegally made from selling merchandise but she also asks the judge to reimburse her for the money that she spent on attorney's fees. She wins the case.

4. You can get international rights. Federal trademarks protect your mark within the United States of America. However, if you decide that you want to protect your mark internationally, you can use the rights that you have as the owner of a federal trademark in the U.S. to help build your legal case to apply for trademark rights in other countries.

Example: *Now that Stacy has a registered trademark in the United States for the name of her nonprofit, she hears that supporters in China have recently discovered her website over the Internet and might also be interested in donating to support her nonprofit. This means that they may also want to purchase items that feature her nonprofit's logo that she has licensed to other vendors.*

In order to protect her brand from knock-off nonprofits in China that may start selling the novelty products her nonprofit has on its website, Stacy hires her attorney to file to register her trademark in China as well as several other major countries. Since she already has acquired or gained the rights to the mark in the United States of America, she uses this as a basis to apply for rights to the mark in

China.

5. Your mark is marketable. A federal trademark is considered intellectual property. This means that oftentimes corporations or foundations that may be interested in sponsoring your nonprofit may want to make sure that you own the rights to your brand before they make a donation. They do not want to risk spending money donating to a nonprofit only for it to be sued by someone else later which is a waste of their resources. Therefore, the mark is something that has value in the market and can be sold.

6. Use the Symbol. Owning a Federal trademark also allows you to use the "Circle-R" or "®" registered trademark symbol. This symbol puts everyone on notice that you are the owner of the mark and that they cannot use it without your permission. If you use the registered trademark symbol without actually having registered your trademark, you can face federal penalties.

Common Law Trademark Rights

Believe it or not, you do not have to actually apply for a federal trademark to begin building legal rights in the name or logo of your nonprofit. Generally, the person that uses the name first "in commerce" has the right to the name as long as no one else used it "in commerce" before you. Using the mark in commerce gives you "common law" rights to the mark.

However, as we have already discussed, one of the main reasons you should still invest in registering your name as a federal trademark - instead of just using it relying on common law rights and hoping no one else does - is that registering the name makes it much easier to legally prove that you are the actual owner of the name.

For example, if you think of a really creative name for your nonprofit or group and start using it without registering it as a federal trademark, someone else in another state can have their lawyer contact you to sue you to stop you from using their name. If they win in court, you can be responsible for money damages.

If you have not registered the name as a federal trademark, you will likely have to hire an attorney to try to gather evidence to build a case to prove that you started using the name before the other user did. This can be an expensive and time-consuming process as you may need to hire expert witnesses, prepared testimony and defend yourself in a court proceeding in order to try to prove that you are entitled to legal ownership of the name. It is basically your word against theirs since you did not register it as a federal trademark. If the other side wins, you could end up paying the original owner and lose the ability to use the name for your nonprofit.

On the other hand, if you take the time to register your name up front as a federal trademark, you can simply let the person know that you are the registered federal trademark owner of the name. This statement alone is oftentimes enough to discourage someone from challenging your legal ownership of a name.

How to Apply for a Federal Trademark

Now that we understand the benefits of having a federal trademark to protect and own your nonprofit's name, let's walk through the specific steps that you will need to take in order to register your nonprofit's name as a federal trademark. My firm has handled this process for clients throughout the country with a 100% success rate since 2010 (Past results do not determine future outcomes).

Here are the steps:

1. Visit www.USPTO.gov

2. Complete the federal trademark application

3. Upload a specimen (sample) of your mark

4. Pay the filing fee (from $250 to $350 depending on which application you choose)

5. Respond timely to the inquiries (called Office Actions) from the USPTO examining attorney with the correct legal responses until they make a final decision regarding your application.

Although the steps appear to be straightforward, the federal trademark process is a very serious undertaking. Generally, only around 41% of applications are approved (Source: the United States Patent & Trademark Office website). Let's unpack the process specifically and discuss what it takes to file.

Completing the Federal Trademark Application

The federal trademark application will require you to provide the following information in order to submit your federal trademark application for consideration:

1. Ownership Information. You will need to list the owner(s) of the mark. The owner(s) can be an individual(s) or a business. During the legal consultation we schedule with clients of our law firm, we carefully analyze their legal and financial situation to let them know if it would be in their best interest to own the trademarks in their name as an individual, in the name of their business or if we need to form a separate holding company for the trademarks. This all depends on a number of factors such as their individual level of exposure to liability, their long-term and short-term goals for the trademarks, tax implications, etc.

2. Contact Information. You will need to provide the USPTO with the primary contact for the application. This information is public record. Most of our clients choose to have our law firm listed as the contact so that they do not have to worry about the examining attorney calling them personally to ask questions about the application while it is under review. Many simply do not want their home address or personal contact information made public. Other clients want to make sure that all official correspondence comes to us so that they are not responsible for missing an important phone call or email from the government which can cause their application to be terminated because they did not respond by the stated deadlines.

3. Drawing / Depiction of the Mark. You will have the choice to register your mark as a "standard character" drawing or as a "special form" drawing. Usually, if you are protecting the name of your nonprofit, you would use a standard character drawing. This means that the words or numbers themselves would be owned by you. For example, the name "Chisholm Law Firm Foundation" would be owned by the nonprofit if they used the standard character drawing.

On the other hand, if you want to own your logo or if the name of your nonprofit's name is written in a special font or design, you would need to file a separate application and choose the special form drawing. Special form drawings, in particular, are governed by very specific rules. I would recommend that you at least speak with a trademark attorney to make sure you are following the guidelines even if you were planning to complete the special form drawing aspect of the application yourself. You can search online for "trademark attorney in Los Angeles" (or insert your city) to find a lawyer in your city. Later in this book, I discuss the things you want to look for when hiring an attorney to help you make a wise decision.

4. Filing Basis. You will have the choice of stating that you are currently using the mark or that you plan on using it in the future. There are specific regulations regarding the criteria you need to meet for each of these. For example, for the "intent to use" filing basis, you must have the good faith intent to actually use the mark. It cannot be something that you plan to register and then never actually use it in commerce. For the "in use" application, you will need to share the actual dates when you first began using the mark in commerce and provide supporting evidence.

5. Goods/Services. You will need to show that you were using your mark (or plan to use it, depending on the filing basis that you choose) with actual goods or services in commerce. This means that if you are filing a trademark application to own your nonprofit's name, you would need to list the services that you will offer when using your nonprofit's name in the marketplace. Lawyers do this by conducting legal research and evaluating the 45 International classes (categories) that the USPTO uses to classify goods and services. You would then find the class or category that includes the charitable services you plan to offer and list it in your application along with a description of the specific services that you offer. You can register to own your name in as many categories as possible. However, there is a separate application fee for each international class (category) that you apply to own your name in.

6. Specimen. You will also need to include a specimen with your application. The drawing that we discussed earlier shows the mark itself (e.g., "Chisholm Law Firm Foundation"). The specimen shows the mark attached to actual goods (e.g., "Chisholm Law Firm Foundation" printed on a T-shirt) if you are applying to own the mark in an international class for apparel.

Can you apply for more than one mark in the same application?

No, you cannot apply for more than one mark in the same application. You can only include one mark (either a name or logo/design) per application. This means that if the name of your nonprofit is "Chisholm Law Firm Foundation" and your logo is an image of the scales of justice, you would need to file one application to own the name of your nonprofit and file a separate second application (and pay a new filing fee) to own your logo.

What is the TEAS Plus application?

Primarily, there are four different application fees based on the type of application you choose. The TEAS Plus application filing fee is $250 per class of goods and or services in the application. This means that if you want to own your name in multiple international classes (categories), you will need to pay $250 per class (category). For example, if you want to own the name of your nonprofit in the educational services category as well as the apparel category to protect your merchandise featuring your nonprofit's name, your filing fee would be $450 ($250 for the educational category plus another $250 for the apparel category). The TEAS Plus application is less expensive than the TEAS regular application because you were limited to describing the goods and services that you offer based on the predefined descriptions included within the USPTO's Acceptable Identification of Goods and Services Manual (ID Manual). For example, your nonprofit may sell limited edition Henley shirts in your online store. The ID manual may not have a predefined description for "henley shirts" so you may have to simply list that you sell "long sleeve shirts" in general.

In addition, you must meet several other requirements in order to qualify for the discounted TEAS Plus application fee:

1. Your application must be complete when you file it since most of the fields in the TEAS Plus application are considered mandatory.

2. You have to identify the goods and services associated with your mark using the USPTO's Acceptable Identification of Goods and Services Manual (ID Manual).

3. You have to pay for all of the international classes associated with your mark when you file the application.

4. You must file the application as well as any future responses electronically using TEAS.

5. You must consent to email communication and submit a working email address.

What is the TEAS Standard Application?

The third type of application is the TEAS Regular application. The filing fee for the TEAS Regular application is $350. This application is more expensive because it allows you to describe the goods and services that you offer without being limited to the predefined descriptions included within the USPTO's Acceptable Identification of Goods and Services Manual (ID Manual). There are few more requirements as well:

1. The applicant must include their name and address.

2. The applicant must submit a clear drawing of the mark.

3. The applicant must list the goods and services associated with the mark.

4. The applicant must submit a filing fee for at least one class of goods or services.

Can you get a refund of your application fees if your filing is rejected?

The electronic trademark applications that are available through the USPTO website give you the opportunity to pay for the filing fee using a major credit card or debit card. Keep in mind that the filing fees are generally non-refundable. This means that you want to have confidence in your understanding of the process (or confidence in the attorney or company you hired) so that you do not have to refile the application multiple times and pay the filing fee multiple times as a result.

How to respond to the government's attorney?

Many people mistakenly think that the application process is complete after you submit your trademark application. This could not be farther from the truth! Instead, one of the most important parts of the application process begins after you have submitted your application. This is the part where you have to respond to the examining attorneys inquiries.

Approximately 3 months after you submit your trademark application, the government will assign an examining attorney to your file. This is the trademark attorney responsible for reviewing your application to see if it meets the federal criteria for trademark registration. This attorney does not represent you but represents the government's interests.

An examining attorney will usually contact you with an Office Action. An Office Action is an official letter from the USPTO examining attorney that may ask questions regarding your application, list additional requirements that you need to meet in order for them to consider approving your registration or may include their reasons for denying your application and give you an opportunity to respond.

Either way, once you have filed your trademark application, it is imperative that you reply to the examining attorney by their deadline. The deadline will always be included in the letter and is usually 3 months from the date, with a possible 3-month extension if you pay a fee. It is your responsibility to keep up with the deadlines and file your responses accordingly. The USPTO will not send you reminders. If you do not respond by the deadline, they may terminate your application and require you to start the entire process over again! This means you have to repay the filing fees because they are non-refundable.

Many of our clients have peace of mind knowing that responses to Office Actions are included in our trademark registration service so they do not have to worry about missing a deadline and losing their trademark rights to someone else.

18 Ways to Overcome a Potential Refusal

Receiving an Office Action from an examining attorney is very serious - but not impossible to overcome. Here are a few ways you can respond to the examining attorney's Office Action and overcome a potential refusal of your registration. Our firm has successfully used many of these strategies to get our clients' trademark applications approved despite intimidating Office Actions:

1. Submit arguments against the refusal.

2. Attach supporting evidence in support of your argument against the refusal.

3. Submit a disclaimer.

4. Submit a stippling statement.

5. Submit a section 2(f) claim.

6. Submit a consent to register names likenesses signatures of individuals.

7. Make a supplemental register Amendment.

8. Make a concurrent use claim.

9. Submit a new drawing of the mark.

10. Submit a better quality image.

11. Pay an additional fee for an existing class.

12. Submit the $50 fee for losing TEAS Plus status.

13. Submit a signed declaration to verify an application.

14. Modify the identification of goods and/or services.

15. Change the filing basis.

16. Add/modify dates of use.

17. Submit a new or substituted specimen.

18. Submit a foreign registration certificate.

Again, if the application is not approved, the government will not provide you with the refund. Therefore, you want to make sure that you are confident in your application as well as your Office Action responses in order to give your trademark the best chance at first-time approval.

How long does it take to know if your application is approved?

From the time you submit your application to the USPTO, it typically takes eight months to a year for you to find out if your trademark was approved. It can sometimes take longer. However, the important thing to know is that the earlier you file your application the better. Filing early should help give you a head start over any competition that may be considering using the same name. This will allow you to have confidence in knowing that you are investing in a brand that you will be able to legally own and are able to legally protect.

How to Hire Help with the Trademark Process

The federal trademark process can be intimidating and there is a lot at stake. There are several internet companies that advertise low fees to complete the process. However, these companies are not attorneys so they cannot legally advise you on the process. They are limited to allow you to fill in your own responses. Many of them rely on applicants making mistakes and having their applications denied. Their hope is to have the applicants re-apply through them

- hence increasing their fees. Not all internet companies are like this - but we have had several clients come to our office after feeling that they were cheated by an online non-lawyer business.

The other alternative is to hire an experienced trademark attorney. For a reasonable fee, an attorney will complete the entire process for you and provide you with the comfort of knowing that it will be filed the right way the first time around. ***Presently, our firm has a 100% success rate with our trademark filings when the national average is only 41% success*** (Source: USPTO website). (Disclaimer: Past results do not determine future outcomes).

Here is a summary of my law firm's trademark process.

1. Comprehensive name search. We research and identify any existing threats to our client's ownership of the mark (e.g. name of their nonprofit, logo or slogan etc.) This includes researching other pending applications as well as any other opposition to the mark. This step is critical because it allows us to let our clients know up front if it will be legally possible for them to own their mark or if someone else already has acquired legal rights to the mark.

If we learn that someone else is already using the mark and has acquired legal rights to the mark, we let our clients know at the very beginning of the process. We didn't give our clients the option to change the mark that we apply for at no additional cost if their first choice is unavailable. This helps our clients avoid wasting money paying the non-refundable filing fee to the USPTO only to have their application rejected.

2. Name Analysis. After we have confirmed that the name is available, we analyze the strength of the mark. This means we evaluate the mark based on the USPTO's criteria in order to know if the application is likely to be approved based on the law. We stay current with the latest trademark laws. If the name does not pass our analysis, we let our clients know ways they can improve the mark in order to increase its chances of approval. Once the mark passes our analysis, we give our clients an official legal opinion with our approval. This gives our clients confidence in the remainder of the application process moving forward since they know that our firm has already legally analyzed the mark and believe that it meets the USPTO criteria based on the current federal trademark laws.

3. Strategic Consultation. Once the mark is approved, we schedule a meeting with our client to discuss the various filing options (e.g., character drawing vs special form drawing, black and white vs color design, intent to use vs commerce filing basis, supplemental vs principal registry, etc.) We listen to our client's goals and make recommendations so that the registration provides maximum legal protection for them and their brand. We also evaluate all 45 of the international classes before recommending the best classification for our client's trademark. We take into consideration the future of our clients brand in order to structure a comprehensive plan to protect the mark even as our clients grow and expand into new markets and industries.

4. Developing Quality Specimen. We provide digitization, adjustment, and compilation of specimen using our state-of-the-art technology and in-house graphic design department in compliance with the strict USPTO requirements. This prevents our clients from having to file multiple trademark applications with the USPTO and paying additional filing fees due to submissions that do not meet the USPTO's specifications.

5. Filing the Application. Once we have completed the above-referenced steps, we file the federal trademark application with the USPTO and provide our client with a copy of the application for their records.

6. Ongoing Legal Representation. We communicate with the USPTO examining attorney throughout the entire application review process by responding to their office actions and answering their questions on behalf of our clients. We also monitor the application to ensure that deadlines are met so that our clients do not have to worry about their application being terminated due to a missed deadline.

7. Trademark Certificate. Once the federal trademark registration is approved, we provide our clients with their official certificate as well as give them instructions regarding maintaining and renewing their trademark registration as needed.

The best news is that our clients are able to deduct 100% of their legal fees on their taxes as a business expense for professional services. If you feel that you may be interested in hiring an attorney to handle the federal trademark application process for you, please be sure to reference the chapter in this book where I specifically discuss the things you want to look for when hiring an attorney.

If you feel we would be a good fit to assist you, feel free to reach out to my office (www.ChisholmFirm.com) and we will provide a Free Trademark Legal Consultation (Value: $450) to see if we're a good fit to work together.

How to protect yourself if someone is using your name?

If you discover that someone else is using the name of your nonprofit, you have several choices.

1. **You can ask them to stop.** You can send an e-mail or a letter letting them know that you have rights in the name and you are asking that they stop infringing on your trademark and stop using the name.

2. **You can ask for their assets.** You can ask them to transfer any web accounts that they are currently using with the name to you. You can request that they transfer the usernames and passwords to their YouTube, Twitter, Facebook, Instagram, etc. accounts if they are using your protected name.

3. **You can hire a lawyer.** If your request is not successful, you can hire an attorney to send a formal legal notice for you. Our firm has been quite successful with these notices as a means of compelling people to stop using our client's intellectual property and having them transfer the accounts back to our clients. Unfortunately, some people will ignore other people but they rarely ignore lawyers since they know a lawyer can force them into court by filing a lawsuit which could result in a judgment against them.

How to respond if you receive a notice that you're using someone's name.

If you are ever in a situation where you receive a notice that you are using someone else's name, you can take the following steps:

1. **Know your rights.** Look the company up online to try and find out when they first started using the name. You also want to know if they are using it for similar products and services as you.

2. **Change the name.** If you do not feel that you have a case (they have been using it before you started in very similar classes or product/service categories), then you may want to change your name as not to infringe on their rights.

3. **Research their registration.** If you feel you may have a case, it may be worth hiring an attorney to research the matter to see if they legally own the name. The attorney can also send them a formal response on your behalf either defending your right to keep using the name or letting them know that you will agree to turn it over to them peacefully.

In this chapter, we've gone into detail about how to legally own your nonprofit's name by registering it as a federal trademark. Now we'll talk about the 10 things you need to do to avoid being sued personally for your nonprofit's actions even if you've incorporated with the state.

Chapter Seven

Chapter 5: 10 Things You Need to Do to Avoid Being Sued Personally for Your Nonprofit's Actions Even If You've Incorporated with the State

A *ccidents happen. My nonprofit's signature event is our annual leadership conference for high school students. One year, in particular, one of our speakers was doing an activity with our students at the conference and asked for a few volunteers to illustrate his point. There were over 100 students in the auditorium and two students volunteered. One student was supposed to attempt to catch a football while the other was supposed to playfully stop them. Instead, the student playing defense accidentally ran directly into the female student that was catching the ball!*

Thankfully, she was all right. She ended up with a small cut on her lip that was bleeding and she was a little shaken up. However, that moment could have had a different outcome and reminded me of just how important it is to have your nonprofit structured properly to minimize liability if things occur. I also learned the importance of informing future speakers that interactive activities involving touch football are strictly prohibited.

Now that we've made sure that you legally own the name of the nonprofit that you will be building a brand around - so that you can avoid trademark infringement lawsuits and the expense of having to start all over with a new name - we can start focusing on the actual legal structure of your nonprofit.

Like we discussed earlier in the book, one of the first ways to reduce your liability when starting your nonprofit is to incorporate your nonprofit. I shared that instead of putting your financial future in jeopardy every time you choose to do something with your nonprofit, you can register your nonprofit by filing the required paperwork with your state and the federal government. If you decide to register your nonprofit, or have already done so, you are taking a step in the right direction toward separating any legal obligations the nonprofit may have from yourself as an individual.

This means that if there was a legal dispute based on something the nonprofit was responsible for doing, the other party likely would not be able to file a lawsuit against you as an individual but would have to sue the nonprofit. The nonprofit would then be responsible for paying any money owed out of the money available in the nonprofit's bank account.

However, even if you've incorporated your nonprofit, the "limited liability" or protection from being personally liable for the debts of the nonprofit is not absolute. For example, intentional and grossly negligent acts are not protected. This means that if you intentionally punch a volunteer at an event hosted for your nonprofit, the volunteer can sue you personally and the nonprofit's limited liability shield will not legally protect you from your actions.

Incorporating your nonprofit is not enough to protect you. You will also need to follow these very specific rules regarding the way you run your nonprofit in order to make sure you do not lose the limited liability protection due to "piercing the corporate veil". Which in essence means that a person violated one or more of these provisions which resulted in a judge ruling that they were not running their nonprofit like a nonprofit, and thus deserve to be penalized as an individual.

The good news is that as long as you do not co-sign or personally guarantee nonprofit debts, here are things you can do to preserve your limited liability protection:

1. File your Annual Report.

You must file an Annual Report with the state you incorporated in each year, typically between January 1st and May 1st of every year, to maintain "active" status. The nonprofit's first annual report will typically be due between January 1st and May 1st of the calendar year following the year the nonprofit is formed and in most states may be filed online. A filing fee is required and some states impose very expensive penalties if it is not filed on time. Many states will send reminders but are not required to do so. You want to make sure you supply a good email address to the state so that you receive their emails if they ever want to send important information with deadlines. My firm always encourages our clients to file early. We even offer an annual subscription service that handles all of the annual filings to make sure they never miss a deadline.

2. File your nonprofit tax return.

Make sure you file your Form 990-N, Form 990 Postcard and/or Form 1023 within the I.R.S. each year. Failing to file this with the I.R.S. can result in you owing taxes and being legally obligated to pay them as your nonprofit will also need to register to pay sales tax if you are selling "unrelated goods" and services. These are services/goods that are not related to your charitable purpose. There are specific rules on this so feel free to reach out to the I.R.S. directly or retain a nonprofit lawyer if you need further assistance

3. Keep Good Records.

Keep your receipts, bank statements, returned checks, contracts, invoices, etc. for your records. We recommend that you invest in financial management software to keep track of your transactions.

4. Don't Mix Your Money.

Open a separate bank account for the nonprofit. Pay yourself in the form of a check instead of making arbitrary cash transfers and withdrawals from your nonprofit account. Pay personal expenses from your personal account. Pay nonprofit expenses from your nonprofit account. If the board decides to make a loan, make a promissory note with interest and write a check payable to your nonprofit. Purchase different color checks to distinguish the two accounts.

5. Sign on Behalf of the Nonprofit.

Avoid signing contracts with your individual name. Instead, use a signature block for any time you are contracting on behalf of the nonprofit:

Chisholm Law Firm Foundation, Inc., nonprofit

By: _____

It's: Executive Director

6. Put it in Writing.

Have written contracts for transactions that plainly state your policies.

7. Write a Resolution.

Document major nonprofit actions by writing a resolution on behalf of the nonprofit ratifying the decision. Keep resolutions in your corporate minute book.

8. Choose nonprofit names carefully.

Avoid forming multiple nonprofits whose names are too similar to your current nonprofit. If you do, you can risk causing your current nonprofit to be held liable for the actions of the other nonprofits. If the nonprofits all share similar management teams, recordkeeping, have similar names, etc., the opposing party could argue that they are merely "alter egos" of the current nonprofit and deserves to share liability.

9. Keep Money in the Nonprofit Account

Make sure you keep sufficient funds in the nonprofit's bank account to meet current obligations and bills – even before paying yourself. Otherwise, the account may be considered undercapitalized which is another legal argument for "piercing the corporate veil" and holding the individuals running the nonprofit responsible for its actions.

10. Vote on Major Decisions.

Make sure you vote as a board before you make major decisions that affect your nonprofit (e.g., hire staff, take out a bank loan, buy property, dissolve the nonprofit, etc.)

Now that we've talked about the 10 things you should do to avoid being sued personally for your nonprofit's actions even if you're incorporated, let's now move forward with a discussion on how to avoid having to pay taxes on your personal tax return for donations received by your nonprofit.

Chapter Eight

Chapter 6: How to Avoid Having To Pay Taxes on Your Personal Tax Return for Donations Received By Your Nonprofit

I *still remember the first major grant I received for Revolution Leadership. It was exciting and intimidating at the same time because I had one big question: How do I report this on my taxes? Or do I even need to report it on my taxes? And if not on my taxes, how do I report it? This chapter will clarify what you need to do to make sure that you don't end up with a tax bill for any donations your nonprofit receives.*

An important benefit of having a properly structured nonprofit is that you will be able to get donations and those donations are tax-deductible. Even if you are planning on funding your nonprofit yourself, this is still a good feature to have because it means that the money that you or your business are donating to keep the nonprofit running will also yield a tax benefit for you.

However, if you do not legally structure your nonprofit the right way you can end up being personally responsible for paying taxes on all of the money and donations that you bring in for your nonprofit. Here is an example:

Example: *Ashton was excited about his nonprofit that would help educate athletes about common health risks associated with their sport and provide them with resources for making healthier decisions. He was posting on social media about his charity and it attracted the attention of a popular professional athlete that liked the nonprofit so much that he shared the post with his followers.*

Without warning, Ashton started receiving donations from complete strangers wanting to support his nonprofit. He hadn't taken the time to set it up properly but figured he would just start using the money toward making a difference. He raised over $100,000 from the social media campaign and used the money to host programs that helped educate hundreds of athletes in his City.

The next year, just as he was planning to reach out to the professional athlete for help again, he received a letter in the mail from the I.R.S. He read the letter and it said that he owed $30,000 in taxes from the previous year from the money he raised for his charity. The worst part about it was he owed the money personally since he *had never taken the time to set up the charity as an organization that was completely separate from himself as an individual.*

By this time, he had already spent all of the money he raised the previous year but was now under pressure to pay the $30,000 or face serious legal penalties- including jail time - if he did not pay or do something to fix the situation.

How do you make sure that you set up your nonprofit so that you do not end up being personally responsible for paying taxes on the money your nonprofit receives as donations? There are a few key legal documents that you will need. Let's talk about them and the things you need to include in each one to legally protect yourself:

1. Articles of Incorporation

Articles of Incorporation help to establish your nonprofit as its own entity so that you are not personally liable for taxes on donations received. Please reference the earlier chapter for a discussion on what needs to be included in your articles of incorporation.

2. Federal Employer Tax Identification Number (FEIN).

The next thing that you need to do is to apply for a Federal Employer Tax Identification Number (FEIN) for your nonprofit. This number is also called an EIN or Tax ID number. I always tell my clients that your FEIN is like a social security number for your nonprofit. If donations that you collect for your nonprofit are linked to your personal social security number, then the I.R.S. will view those donations as personal income to you and they will want you to pay taxes for them personally as an individual. This is not what you want to happen because that income is not for your personal use. It was given to your nonprofit and is for use by your nonprofit and should be tax exempt.

The FEIN also allows your nonprofit to be responsible for any taxes it owes. For example, if you received any "unrelated business income" or money from activities that are not related to furthering your tax-exempt purposes, your nonprofit is able to pay these taxes separately from your personal taxes using this number.

My law firm obtains FEINs for our clients online because they're able to receive their number and begin using it immediately. Here is how you apply:

How to apply for a FEIN online:

1. Make sure you qualify.

○ Is your nonprofit in the U.S. or a U.S. territory?

○ Do you as the applicant have a valid social security number, taxpayer identification number or federal employer identification number?

○ Have you already legally formed your nonprofit first? You'll want to make sure you've done this first because getting your FEIN will trigger the time frame for your annual filings being due. If you don't file them for 3 years in a row, you'll lose your tax exempt status so only apply once you're legally formed.

2. Fill out the online application

○ Go to

○ Search for "federal employer identification number" and you should be able to find a link to apply for a tax ID number.

○ Fill out the application (Remember to do it all at once because you can't save it or pick up where you left off if you haven't used the site for 15 minutes

○ Submit the Application online

3. Save your paperwork

○ Download the application and your assigned tax identification number and save them for your records.

Now that you have your federal employer tax identification number, you want to make sure that everything you do on behalf of your nonprofit is associated with that number, not your personal social security number. For example, when you open a bank account, when you apply for a loan for the charity, when you apply for grants, etc. You will want them to all list the federal employer identification number for your nonprofit.

Filing your Articles of Incorporation with the state as well as applying for a Federal Employer Identification Number are two things that will help to ensure that you do not end up being personally liable for taxes based on donations received from the nonprofit. Now, let's talk about ways you can protect your privacy when starting your nonprofit.

Chapter 7: How to Protect Your Privacy When Forming Your Nonprofit

We live in a digital world that has allowed people from all over the world to connect and have access to your information. As such, it makes sense to be concerned about privacy and protecting your identity even when forming your nonprofit. Here are just a few ways that you can protect your privacy which in turn protect your identity from identity theft as you are forming your nonprofit.

1. Protecting your home address

One of the things you will be required to do in order to legally form your nonprofit as well as for future paperwork in relation to your nonprofit is to provide a mailing address and a physical address.

The mailing address requirement refers to an address where you will receive mail for the nonprofit. If you can afford it, you can open a post office box and receive mail relating to your nonprofit at that address. This is often a good option because your mail is under lock and key and is separate from the personal mail that you received directly at your home. This can make it easier to stay organized and keep up with important paperwork that relates to your nonprofit.

The other requirement on the paperwork necessary to legally form your nonprofit will be providing a physical address. This needs to be an actual location where the nonprofit maintains a physical presence. It cannot just be a box where mail is received. You have a few options.

1. Buy or Lease an Office. The option to buy a commercial storefront door building or even lease office space for your nonprofit is ideal. The downside is that this is a huge expense for a new nonprofit and other more cost-efficient options may be worth considering depending on your budget.

2. Use your office. You can use the address of an office location that you have access to and permission to use. For example, if you own a small business, you can use that mailing address. Or, if you have a key donor or supporter that owns an office, you can ask if they will sponsor your nonprofit by allowing you to receive mail at their location and or use office space at their location for meetings on occasion.

3. Home Address of Board Member or Supporter. If one of the board members of your nonprofit is comfortable with using their home address, you can use that address. You just want to make sure that you first have permission to list the address but also that whoever gets the mail for that address will be responsible enough to provide it to you in a timely fashion just in case something important arrives that you need to handle.

4. Virtual Office - many companies will allow you to use the physical address of their office building as well as have occasional access to the building for meetings for a flat monthly fee or a per-use fee. This may be a good option for your nonprofit if you have a modest budget but still want a professional public appearance for your organization. Feel free to do an online search for the word "virtual office" in your city to see a list of options and prices.

5. Suite Address for PO Box - there are also private companies that offer Post Office boxes but provide a physical address for the Box. This may be a good option for you. You will, of course, need to check with the requirements of your state to see if this is permitted. Some post offices will also allow you to use the physical address of their location with your post office box listed as a suite. Again, check with your State's requirements to see if this is an option for you.

6. Your Home Address. The last option is to use your actual home address. Keep in mind that this address will be listed on the public record and may remain on public record even after you have changed the address in the future. It may be worth the modest investment to consider one of the above-mentioned options if protecting your privacy is a concern.

2. Protecting your phone number

Many of the legal documents that you are required to complete as well as subsequent documents for your nonprofit such as bank accounts, grant applications, etc. may require that you include a phone number for your nonprofit. I strongly encourage you to get a separate number for your nonprofit instead of using your cell phone number. Getting a separate number for your nonprofit accomplishes several things.

First, it protects your privacy from the general public. Second, it allows your nonprofit to have the look and feel of a professionally run organization. Third, it can help you stay organized as it relates to opportunities and responsibilities for your nonprofit. For example, you can check the dedicated voicemail for your nonprofit and stay on top of calls you need to return instead of those important calls being lost amidst your personal calls and voicemails on your personal cell phone.

There are a few ways to protect your personal phone number.

1. Call Forwarding

You can pay for or use a free call forwarding service. This will give you a new dedicated telephone number for your nonprofit. The benefit is that calls will still forward directly to your cell phone. Some will even require that the caller identify themselves so that you can choose if you want to take the call or not. You can research paid services such as eVoice or consider free services such as Google Voice.

2. Live Receptionist

Another option is to hire a service to be a live receptionist. Instead of having to pay a full time or part time annual salary plus benefits to a receptionist to answer all of your calls - you can use a call center that will answer calls for you. Instead of paying for an employee, you're only paying for the number of calls that are answered. The receptionist is able to gather information from the caller and will then typically text or email you a summary of each call so that you can call them back. They can even connect you to the caller if you want to speak to them immediately. If you search online for "live receptionist" you can view different company offerings and compare which one works for you.

3. Protect your email address

Instead of using your personal email account, consider setting up an entirely separate nonprofit account for your nonprofit. You can contact your domain name registrar to purchase an email address with the same ending as your website. For example, the name of the nonprofit I started is Revolution Leadership. Our email addresses for the nonprofit all end with "@revolutionleadership.org." Not only does this protect your privacy, but it gives your nonprofit a more professional look and feel to the general public when they are considering you for programs, services as well as funding.

4. Private domain registration

If you're planning on having a website for your nonprofit, you will need to register your information as the owner of the domain where your site is hosted. ICANN, the organization that maintains databases for the internet, requires that the domain name owner's information is listed. This means that anyone can do a "who is" online search and have immediate access to the name, phone number and email address of the person that owns the particular domain. This is one of the reasons why you may want to consider purchasing private domain registration when you buy your domain name. Of course, it does cost more money. Most providers require that you pay for the service annually or monthly. The benefit is that it hides your identifying information so that a stranger online that is trying to locate you will not be able to see your identity.

The downside to purchasing a private domain registration, in addition to the cost, is that the generic company that will be listed as the registered owner for the protection of your privacy is technically the legal owner of the domain. In the event that you were in a legal dispute with them for ownership, this could be an issue.

For information on purchasing a private domain registration, contact your website domain registrar (e.g., godaddy.com, etc.)

5. Registered Agent

In order to form your nonprofit, you will also be required to list a registered agent. The registered agent (RA) is responsible for accepting "service of process" (the legal paperwork that must be hand delivered if the nonprofit is ever sued) and delivering that paperwork to the officers of the nonprofit. Many nonprofits founders list themselves as the registered agent. If you are concerned about protecting your privacy, here are a few other solutions to consider:

1. Friend or Family Member - You can ask a friend or family member if you can list them as the registered agent of your nonprofit. They would need to sign the Articles of Incorporation stating that they are agreeing to accept responsibility as the registered agent. You can also ask board members or stakeholders to serve in this capacity. Keep in mind that registered agents must be a resident of the state you are filing in and must have a physical address in that state. Make sure they meet these two criteria before asking them.

2. Hire a Registered Agent - You can pay a registered agent service for less than $199/year and they will provide you with the address to list. Same process. They would need to sign the

Articles of Incorporation stating that they are agreeing to accept responsibility as the registered agent. We offer this service for clients that want to protect their privacy and don't want to ever be embarrassed by being served lawsuit papers while spending time with friends and family.

3. Serve as the Registered Agent Yourself - You can serve as the registered agent of your nonprofit yourself if you incorporate your nonprofit in the state of your residency. At minimum, we would recommend using one of the privacy strategies shared earlier to protect your home physical address if you choose to serve in this capacity.

In this chapter, we've covered many of the privacy strategies you can use to protect your privacy when you form your nonprofit. Now, let's talk about how to legally structure your nonprofit to avoid trouble with the I.R.S.

Chapter Ten

Chapter 8: How to Legally Structure Your Nonprofit to Avoid I.R.S. Trouble

T he most important part of the legal structure of your 501c3 nonprofit will come in the form of the completion of the Form 1023 Application for Tax Exempt Status. The Application for Tax Exempt Status is the application you are required to complete (with some exceptions) if you want 501c3 tax exempt status for your nonprofit. The way that you choose to complete this form and structure your nonprofit will make a difference as to your ability to qualify for major grant funding, ability to pay staff, ability to pay yourself a salary, etc.

Like most regulatory agencies, the I.R.S. has priorities when it comes to evaluating your nonprofit's Application for Tax Exempt status. In my years of successfully filing the form and obtaining approvals for my clients, I believe the main concerns of the

I.R.S. involve (1) avoiding conflicts of interest; and (2) avoiding nonprofits that only benefit the directors or officers.

In this chapter, I will share how these two priorities are reflected in the various aspects of the Form 1023 Application for Tax Exempt status as well as ways that you can overcome scrutiny. For purposes of this chapter, we will focus on the long form but many of these principles apply to the expedited Form 1023 form as well.

Selecting Board Members, Trustees & Officers

The first area that we will talk about that you can focus on to avoid trouble with the I.R.S. when structuring your nonprofit relates to choosing your board members and officers.

Let's first establish the difference between your board of directors (also referred to as trustees) and your nonprofit's officers.

In general, board members work collectively while officers are individuals that are appointed with specific authority for specific roles. For example, most board of directors focus on establishing the overall goals of the organization and then meet regularly to oversee the work of the officers in order to make sure the nonprofit is focusing on its mission.

On the other hand, officers handle the day to day operations of the nonprofit and are either elected or appointed by the board. Typical nonprofit officer titles include: President, Vice President, Secretary, and Treasurer.

When you are structuring your nonprofit, these are the key relationships that the I.R.S. is concerned about when it comes to individuals serving on the board of directors of your nonprofit:

1. Family Relationships

2. Business Relationships

3. Related (through family or business) to highly paid employees or independent contractors

If you have a relationship with a board member that falls into one of the categories mentioned above, you may need to be prepared to disclose the relationship to the I.R.S. and in some instances explain the nature of the relationship, depending on which form you file when starting your nonprofit. In some instances, I have seen the I.R.S. refuse to grant tax-exempt status to an otherwise qualified organization because their board of directors was comprised entirely of family members.

It may also help to conduct a background check and get references for individuals that you plan to invite to serve on the board. The I.R.S. does not require this but these individuals will be the public face of your nonprofit and it is important that their reputations are appropriate for the type of work your nonprofit is doing. For example, if your nonprofit is advocating for children's safety from abusive homes, it may not be in your best interest to have a board member that is a convicted felon for child abuse.

Again, you can avoid the appearance of a conflict of interest or self-serving board by having a diverse board of individuals and being prepared to disclose any conflicts to the I.R.S.

Paying Employees

Another area of concern for the I.R.S. is how your nonprofit chooses to pay people. The way that you structure your nonprofit as it relates to paying your employees is critical to avoiding trouble with the I.R.S. Here are some things you may want to implement in order to pass I.R.S. muster:

1. Create a conflict of interest policy;

2. Have your board vote and pass a conflict of interest resolution adopting the policy;

3. Appoint a Compensation Committee that will research similar for-profit and nonprofit organizations that offer similar services, current salary surveys compiled by independent firms, or actual written offers from similar organizations;

4. Document the resources the Compensation Committee used to determine reasonable compensation based on fair market value;

5. Have the board of directors vote to approve pay as recommended by the Compensation Committee before you issue the first paycheck;

6. Have a written employment agreement that documents the agreed-upon terms for pay;

7. Have written meeting minutes that document the vote of each individual on the board as it relates to the pay; and

8. Do not pay staff discretionary or non-fixed payments. If you're going to give bonuses, they shouldn't be based on discretion but rather on a predetermined chart.

If you're not doing all of the above, you'll need to be prepared to explain to the I.R.S. your process for paying staff including how you will decide how much they will be paid and how you'll make sure the pay is to be reasonable.

Purchasing From Vendors

It is perfectly normal for your nonprofit to need to buy goods and services from vendors. The I.R.S. wants to ensure that you will have a process for making reasonable purchases, instead of paying exorbitant amounts of nonprofit funds to support the businesses of board members, officers or even your own family members and friends. Here are a few ways you can structure your nonprofit to safeguard against those types of abuses that may raise a red flag with the I.R.S.:

1. To avoid the appearance of conflicts of interests, you can always choose to buy goods and services for your nonprofit from outside third parties.

2. If you decide to buy goods and services for your nonprofit from any of your nonprofit's officers, directors, employees or independent contractors, you will need to tell the I.R.S. (1) what you are planning to buy; (2) whom you're going to buy it from; (3) how will you make sure the deal is negotiated at arm's length and (4) how you'll make sure you're not paying more than fair market value.

3. Have a policy to require written contracts from vendors and provide a copy to the I.R.S. with your application if available.

4. As a best practice, you may not want to enter into a lease agreement, contract, loan or other agreements with any of your directors, officers or staff. If you do, be prepared to disclose the above-mentioned information to the I.R.S.

5. If you are entering into agreements with any of your highest paid staff or highest paid independent contractors, you will also need to disclose information as the I.R.S. wants to make sure that your entire nonprofit is not designed to benefit these parties since they are already being highly paid by your nonprofit.

Again, it may also be helpful to attach copies of the contracts and agreements to speed up the review process.

Political Involvement

Another area that attracts I.R.S. scrutiny for 501c3 nonprofit applicants is political involvement. Here are the three main activities that will attract attention from the I.R.S. regarding your Application for Tax Exemption:

1. Supporting or opposing candidates in **political campaigns**
2. Attempting to **influence legislation**
3. Legislative activity

If you are planning to do any of the things listed above, you'll need to tell the I.R.S. in detail if your efforts at changing legislation are a substantial part of your activities. This is measured by how much time you are spending as well as how much money you are spending on lobbying compared with everything else you are doing overall.

Bingo and Gaming Activities

Here are three other activities that may raise "red flags" to the I.R.S. as it relates to your 501c3 nonprofit:

1. Bingo activities
2. Gaming activities
3. Hiring other people or organizations to offer bingo or gaming activities for you

If you want to structure your 501c3 nonprofit to engage in any of these activities, you'll need to include the following if you want to avoid issues with the I.R.S.:

• List the income you make from the activities (or project what you expect to make)

● List the expenses you paid from the activities (or project what you anticipate owing)

● If you're hiring someone, you'll need to share how the arrangement is structured. Make sure you include the following:

○ Share how you plan to negotiate at "arm's length"

○ List their salary or wage for the work they are going to perform

○ Share how they will be chosen among other applicants

○ Share that you will research the fair market rate to pay a person in this position to make sure that they are not being overpaid

○ Include a copy of your contract with the person for the I.R.S. to review

Fundraising Activities

The specific fundraising activities that you engage in or plan to engage in are also of particular interest to the I.R.S. Here are some best practices to consider:

1. If you hire someone to fundraise for you, you'll need to share the income and expenses from their work, share who is doing the fundraising for you and provide a copy of the contract to the I.R.S. for review.

2. If you're going to fundraise for other organizations, you'll need to share with the I.R.S. what you're planning to do, whom you're going to do it for and once again attach a copy of the agreement.

3. If you're going to give donors the option to tell you how they want their donation spent, you'll need to let the I.R.S. know that you are going to (1) keep separate accounts for any donor that has

the right to tell you how to use the funds; (2) let the I.R.S. know if the donor will have a say in the investments and distributions of the funds from their particular account; (3) provide specifics regarding the donor's level of involvement with giving advice as well as a copy of the documentation that you give to the donor.

In addition to these main areas, if your nonprofit will be working with Managers, Developers, Joint Ventures and Partnerships, if you are starting a Childcare Organization, Cooperative service organization, Charitable Risk Pool, starting a School, Opening a Hospital or Offering Medical Care, providing Housing for low-income, the elderly or handicapped, Offering Scholarships, Fellowships, Student Loans or Grants, operating in foreign country, etc., you will need to provide additional disclosures and carefully structure your organization as to position yourself to pass I.R.S. scrutiny. An extensive discussion of these activities exceeds the scope of this book. However, if you are considering any of these structures and need assistance, my law firm works one-on-one with clients opening these types of nonprofits and handles all of the paperwork necessary to put them in the best position to be approved by the I.R.S.

Now that we covered how to legally structure your nonprofit to avoid I.R.S. trouble, let's talk about how to avoid getting kicked off of your own board of directors.

Chapter Eleven

Chapter 9: How to Avoid Getting Kicked Off Your Own Board of Directors

I still remember leaving the movie theatre with my husband and hearing people in the lobby of the theatre discussing the latest news. A very well-known nonprofit in our city had voted to kick the co-founder off of the board of directors. There are many instances when removing a board member is merited. However, in this specific instance, it was disheartening because everyone in the community knew that this particular co-founder had an excellent reputation, had helped build the nonprofit from the ground up and was not to blame for their recent struggles.

As a nonprofit attorney, I have represented clients in similar situations. In this chapter, we will explore the role of the board of directors and discuss ways that founders can protect themselves through preventative measures if they are concerned about being wrongfully removed by their board of directors.

Responsibilities of Board Members

Before we can have a meaningful discussion on protecting yourself as a founder from being wrongfully removed from the board, we should begin with an understanding as to the role of the board of directors.

Since nonprofits serve the public, they are governed by a board of directors. The founder of the nonprofit will initially invite individuals to serve on the board. From there, the nonprofit will establish guidelines for electing, removing and replacing board members and outline these procedures in their Bylaws.

Before you invite someone to serve on the board of a nonprofit, or before you agree to serve on a board, it's important to know what is expected and what the responsibilities are that come with the position.

Here is a brief summary of the role of the board of directors:

Roles and Responsibilities of Board Members:

1. Attending board meetings;

2. Participating in committee work;

3. Strategic planning (defining mission and goals of the organization, review programs, funding needs, etc.);

4. Fiduciary responsibilities (approving the annual budget, controlling investment policies, managing capital and reserve funds);

5. Program oversight and support (evaluating all programs and staff. Being an advocate in the community); and

6. Fundraising (contributing personally, identifying and

soliciting contributions from prospective donors and supporters).

Legal Responsibilities of Board Members

1. Act In Good Faith - not doing things that will hurt the nonprofit;

2. Duty of Care - acting reasonably as it relates to the nonprofit;

3. Duty of Loyalty - putting the best interests of the nonprofit first;

4. Confidentiality - Not sharing sensitive information about the nonprofit with outside parties; and

5. Non-competition - not engaging in activities that compete with the nonprofit or undermine its mission.

A helpful practice is to host a Board Orientation and provide each of your directors with a written Board of Directors Manual. We prepare these for our clients so that they don't have to reinvent the wheel and spend unnecessary time writing one. At a minimum, the Board of Directors Manual should include the following information:

Board Manual Table of Contents:

1. Welcome letter from the President

2. Board Member Information Sheet

3. Information about the organization

a. History

b. Mission & Vision

c. Corporate Structure

4. Roles and Responsibilities of Board Members

5. Legal Duties of Board Members

a. Board meetings

b. Committee work

c. Strategic planning

    d. Fiduciary Responsibilities

    e. Program Oversight and Support

    f. Fundraising

    g. Annual Planning

6. Programming Plan (Summer Retreat)

7. Fundraising Plan, Investment Plan & Annual Budget

8. Public Relations Plan

9. Marketing Plan

10. Strategic Plan

Founder's Protection Bylaws™

Let me set the scene. A devoted nonprofit founder sacrifices and spends thousands of dollars of their own money starting a nonprofit to help battered women. They care deeply about the cause and never ask for anything in return. Instead, they hire a top nonprofit attorney to build a world-class organization with a sustainable funding model comprised of passionate donors, a team of dedicated employees and an annual operating budget of $1 million dollars in just a few years.

The founder has never taken a salary but at this point presents to the board a proposal for a modest $150,000 a year annual salary plus benefits. This salary is still competitive considering the unique skills the founder has acquired from working with their nonprofit attorney to learn how to start and grow the nonprofit. The salary represents fair market value for a nonprofit executive with the founder's experience, management, and fundraising ability.

One of the board members becomes jealous of the founder and decides to organize a coup d'etat to kick the founder off of the board so that they can get the salary and run the organization instead. Their efforts succeed, the founder was voted off of the board and the organization continued under the new leadership.

This unfortunate story, although fictional, has happened to good intentioned nonprofit founders over the years. As I stated earlier, there are instances when a founder's removal from the board is merited. That is a discussion for another time. This chapter is focusing on avoiding unwarranted removals of nonprofit founders.

One way that nonprofit founders can avoid this from happening is to ensure that their nonprofit is structured in a way that protects their interests as well as that of the nonprofit. Most nonprofits outline their structure via their Bylaws. Traditional bylaws include the following provisions:

- The number of board members;
- Process for election and removal of officers and board members;
- Process for filling vacancies on the board;
- Requirements for how many meetings must take place, their location, etc.;
- Requirements for how many board members must be in attendance in order to have quorum (number of people required for a meeting to be valid);
- If the nonprofit is dissolved, assets will be donated to a 501c3 organization pursuant to the I.R.S. code;

My law firm offers our clients the option to have proprietary bylaws we've created called Founders Protection Bylaws™ drafted. Founders Protection Bylaws include, but are not limited to, the following provisions:

- The nonprofit is structured to be a membership organization;

- The only member is the founder or incorporator of the nonprofit;

- Despite the existence of a traditional board and officers, the founder can appoint and remove officers & directors at any time with or without cause; and

- The founder can overrule any vote, decision or recommendation by the Board of Directors including budget decisions.

The purpose of this legal structure is not for abuse that they should continue to rely on the advice and counsel of the board. The goal is for them to never need to rely upon the provisions within their bylaws. However, in the unfortunate event that they are in a situation similar to the scenario described at the beginning of this chapter - they will be empowered to evoke the provisions listed in order to protect the overall well-being of the nonprofit.

Thankfully, since nonprofits are public charities, there are regulations based on the I.R.S. Code as well as state and federal law that hold founders accountable in the event that they abuse their role. We always advise our clients that they are still required to abide by criminal and civil laws despite any legal protections we include when structuring their nonprofit.

Now that we have talked about the role of the board of directors and ways that founders can protect themselves from being wrongfully removed from the board, let's discuss how to avoid liability when raising money for a nonprofit.

Chapter Twelve

Chapter 10: How to Avoid Liability When Raising Money for Your Nonprofit

*T*he first major donation I received for Revolution Leadership was a $3000 check from a gentleman I did not know previously but was moved by our story and the work that we were doing for students. Social media makes it easier than ever to get the word out about what you are doing and reach people that are passionate enough about your cause to give. I've made a simple Facebook post that resulted in a $500 donation from one individual that I had never spoken to about my charity nor had I ever asked them to make a donation. Keep in mind that there are pitfalls associated with accepting donations. Here are just a few things to watch out for when raising money for your nonprofit.

Fundraising Registration (Solicitation Licenses)

Raising money has always been a potential source of liability for nonprofit organizations. Here are the general things you need to know. Generally speaking, if your 501c3 nonprofit wants to ask people or organizations in a particular state for donations, you will need to register in that state to "solicit" for donations if they require solicitation or fundraising registration.

Currently, there are 40 states that require fundraising registration. (These are the states that do not have this requirement: Wyoming, Arizona, Vermont, Delaware, Texas, Idaho, South Dakota, Indiana, Nebraska, Iowa, Montana). Unfortunately, there isn't a national registry, so you have to register in each state individually.

The good news is that if you have a new nonprofit – you may be exempt from the requirement in many states if your revenue is under $25,000. But each state's requirements are different.

You typically have to renew the Solicitation License or Fundraising Registration with each state every year. For example, in Florida, the Solicitation License is filed with the Florida Department of Agriculture and Consumer Services Division of Consumer Services and the expiration date for charitable organizations and sponsors is one (1) year from the initial date of compliance with registration requirements.

If your nonprofit plans to raise money in other states, you should consider speaking with a nonprofit attorney about registering in those states to make sure that you are in compliance with the law.

Website Disclaimer when Tax Exempt Status Is Pending

Another source of liability when starting a nonprofit involves receiving donations before you have received your tax exempt status from the I.R.S. If you are collecting donations before having your tax-exempt status from the I.R.S., you may want to include a disclaimer so that donors are aware that your status is pending until approved by the I.R.S. Here is some sample language you can consider using:

Revolution Leadership, Inc. is a registered nonprofit organization. Our application for tax-exemption has been filed and our 501c3 tax-exempt status is currently "pending."

This disclaimer is important because you don't want your donors to feel like you're being untruthful with them. Letting them know that you are still waiting for your tax-exempt status to be approved is not only honest - but also puts them on notice that there is a chance they will not get the tax write-off if you are not approved.

Keep in mind that my law firm typically recommends that our clients wait until they've been approved by the I.R.S. Otherwise if they accept donations and ultimately are not approved - they could be personally responsible for paying taxes on all of the donations they received.

Website Disclaimer When Tax Exempt Status Is Approved

Once your tax-exempt status is approved by the I.R.S., you can use the following language on your website:

Revolution Leadership, Inc. is a federally recognized 501c3 tax-exempt nonprofit organization. As such, donations are tax-deductible to the fullest extent of the law.

This is standard language that you can use on your website to let donors and prospective stakeholders know that they can get a tax write-off for donating to your charity.

General Data Protection Regulation (GDPR) Compliance

In 2018, the European Union passed a law called the "General Data Protection Regulation" (GDPR). The GDPR lets the European Union issue fines to companies and nonprofits that don't follow certain policies as it relates to using private citizens' information.

You will want to make sure your website is GDPR compliant and has the appropriate notices. My law firm prepares GDPR Terms of Use for our nonprofit client's websites. These terms address the issues presented by the GDPR to make sure our clients are in compliance. Once drafted, the Terms can be used for other websites as well.

When to Register Your Nonprofit to Do Business in Other States

Once you have started your nonprofit in one state, you may need to register it as a "foreign corporation" to operate in other states. Generally, there are three primary reasons why a nonprofit may need to register in another state:

1. Nonprofit Operations

If your nonprofit is operating in another state, it may need to register as a "foreign corporation" so that it can get a "certificate of authority" to legally do business in that state.

If you want to know if the work that you are doing with your nonprofit qualifies as operating in another state, the state will look at the following factors: (1) if your nonprofit has an office or employee in that state; (2) if your nonprofit has a physical presence (3) if a substantial part of your nonprofit operations take place in that state; or (4) if your nonprofit has a substantial connection to the state.

Generally, if you're only fundraising across or engaging in an isolated activity, that is not enough to qualify as operating within the state for the purpose of having to register in that state.

2. Fundraising

If your nonprofit is asking for donations within a certain state, some states will require that you register for a solicitation license in addition to the 501c3 approval that you've already obtained from the I.R.S. If the state that you're raising money in requires it, you will need to file a solicitation license in that state as described in the section on Fundraising Registration in this book.

3. Buying Items

If your nonprofit is buying items in another state and wants the order to be exempt from sales tax, the nonprofit may have to apply for a "Sales and Use Tax Exemption." if their I.R.S. Letter of Determination is not enough for that particular store or vendor.

Now that we have learned about ways to stay out of legal trouble when raising money, let's explore the things you should do before accepting major donations to be in compliance with the law.

Chapter Thirteen

Chapter 11: Three Things You Should Do Before Accepting Major Donations

A good way to protect yourself and the reputation of your nonprofit is to make sure you are handling donations that you receive for your nonprofit properly. Here are three things you should do before accepting major donations:

Donor Contribution Statements

The I.R.S. only requires that you give a contribution statement to donors that make a donation of over $250. If you are able, I recommend that you issue donor contribution statements for all donations. Here are a few reasons why this may be a helpful practice for you.

First, providing a Donor Contribution Statement documents

that the amount received was a donation and that there is no expectation of goods and services in exchange for the amount. Although this should be clear when someone gives, it never hurts to put it in writing just in case it is not.

Secondly, a written Contribution Statement conveys your appreciation for the donation. In the Contribution Statements we include in our packages for our clients, we always include language that shares the nonprofit's heartfelt appreciation for the donation.

Lastly, a written Contribution Statement is an opportunity for you to highlight recent accomplishments and describe the impact your nonprofit is making as a result of their contribution. This serves a two-fold purpose. First, it allows the donor to know that they are supporting an organization that is winning and actually executing its mission successfully as reflected in the accomplishments you share in the contribution statement. Secondly, they are able to see that their funds are being well spent which will hopefully encourage them to donate again in the future.

Donor Receipt

Another best practice is to always provide donors with a receipt after they make a donation. Generally, if they donate through PayPal or other merchant processors, the website will automatically generate a receipt and provide it to them electronically. For accounting purposes, having a receipt on file will help you have accurate records as it relates to the actual funds that were received by your nonprofit as well as the sources of those funds.

Donor Agreement

If a donor ever approaches you and wants to make a major gift, I would highly recommend that you consider having a nonprofit attorney prepare a Donor Agreement. A Donor Agreement is a legal contract that outlines the terms of a charitable gift. It will lay out the rules for the donation and also make sure that both parties are in compliance with the law. A donor agreement is absolutely critical if the major gift comes with any types of restrictions or stipulations.

My law firm drafts Donor Agreements for clients all of the time. They help the parties to avoid misunderstandings. They are specifically designed to discourage the donor from later requesting their money back or claiming that they are owed certain benefits or services in exchange for the gift - even if such terms were never apart of the original understanding. Trust me, these things do happen, so it is well worth it to legally protect yourself and have a signed Donor Agreement in place for major donations.

Accepting Donations When Something Was Given in Exchange For the Donation

There is another important rule that you need to know when it comes to accepting donations. If your nonprofit gives a donor a good or service in conjunction with their donation to your nonprofit, this is called a **Quid Pro Quo Contribution.** In these instances, only the amount over the fair market value is tax-deductible.

Keep in mind that your nonprofit is required to pay taxes on any income it receives that is not substantially related to your nonprofit's exempt purposes. This is called the **Unrelated Business Income.** If you will be offering goods or services, make sure you speak with a nonprofit attorney first to make sure you structure things so that you are in compliance with the I.R.S.

Example: Ashton decides to sell his signature cupcakes as a fundraiser to benefit his nonprofit. He wants the people that buy his cupcakes to be able to get a tax deduction for buying the cupcakes because his 501c3 nonprofit is selling them.

After speaking with his nonprofit attorney, she shared that the amount that customers pay above fair market value is the amount that they can write off on their taxes since they are getting something in exchange for a donation.

With this information in mind, Ashton knew that the cost of a gourmet cupcake similar to his in his city was $4. He decided to charge $5.50 for his cupcakes. This means that with each cupcake purchase, his customers would be able to write off $1.50 on their taxes since this is the amount that they "donated" to the nonprofit above and beyond the actual fair market value of the cupcake they received.

How to Know How Much Someone Can Write Off on Their Taxes

As you are talking to donors about giving to your nonprofit, you will most likely get lots of questions. A popular question may be the donor wanting to know exactly how much they can write off on their taxes.

As a general rule, you can let donors know that donations to your charity are 100% tax-deductible to the fullest extent of the law - assuming you have obtained your 501c3 tax exempt status from the I.R.S. I do advise that you still encourage donors to consult with their accountant regarding the specific tax benefits they are eligible to receive since the tax code changes every year. Unless you are a tax professional, you don't want to be held responsible for giving them inaccurate information. Here are a few general guidelines that are valid as of the date of this publication that you may find helpful:

1. Individual Donations - In general, individual donations to charitable organizations may be deducted up to 50% of the person's adjusted gross income. If a person donates more than 50% of their adjusted gross income, the excess may be carried forward for up to five years.

2. Business Donations - If a business makes a charitable donation, the I.R.S. will generally classify it as a personal expense and the corporation cannot deduct it as a business expense. Instead, it would be viewed as an itemized tax deduction. Again, the business should consult with a certified public accountant to review the schedules it files for its taxes to find out how to maximize tax benefits relating to the gift.

Now that we have discussed the things you should do to legally protect your nonprofit when accepting major donations, let's learn how to avoid financial scandals when handling money for your nonprofit.

Chapter Fourteen

Chapter 12: How to Avoid Financial Scandals When Handling Money for Your Nonprofit

*A*lmost everyone at some point has felt the feeling of disappointment when listening to the news and hearing about yet another nonprofit scandal. The good news is that this does not have to be your story. There are plenty of successful nonprofits that have been able to operate and enjoy good reputations while remaining above reproach. You can as well! Let's talk about some concepts that will assist you in avoiding financial scandals when handling money for your nonprofit.

Profit doesn't belong to you. If you can embrace this concept, you will be able to avoid a lot of misfortune as it relates to your 501c3 nonprofit. Although nonprofits can be profitable - the profit does not belong to you. For example, if you offer inexpensive private tutoring services targeted at low-income families and still end up with $50,000 remaining, that "profit" does not belong to you. You would need to reinvest those funds into furthering the charitable purpose of the nonprofit.

For example, instead of paying yourself the $50,000 outright by writing yourself a check, you could instead propose that the board of directors increase your salary by $50,000 for the following year. This would work if the new increased salary amount would be considered "reasonable compensation" based on the other factors listed in the chapter of this book that discusses executive compensation.

Don't Abuse Tax Incentives. As a 501c3 tax-exempt nonprofit organization, you will have the luxury of being exempt from federal taxes when making purchases. If you want to avoid financial scandals, you will need to make sure you are not abusing those tax incentives.

Example: Justin wanted to host a launch party for his new tech company. He realized that his funds were low after having spent most of his budget on computers, servers, and equipment for the business. Instead of reducing the budget or waiting to have the event when he could afford it, he decided to wrongfully use his tax-exempt certificate to buy everything for his party. This allowed him to save money by not having to pay sales taxes on any of the decorations, equipment rental, catering costs, venue fees, etc. Since the launch party was not related to his exempt purposes, he is now in violation of federal law.

The same rule applies as it relates to letting other people use your nonprofit's tax-exempt certificate to make purchases that are unrelated to your charity's mission.

Avoid Excess Benefit. Generally speaking, the Excess Benefit Transaction rule means that you shouldn't pay someone unreasonably more compensation than they deserve for the work they've done. In order to avoid violating this rule, it may be a good idea to reference the chapter in this book on executive compensation. In this chapter, I explain the steps you should take to research and make sure a proposed salary is reasonable based on I.R.S. recommendations.

Three Primary Ways Fraud Occurs in Nonprofits

In addition to the three concepts I just shared, here are three primary ways that fraud occurs in nonprofits:

1. Embezzlement - Someone within the organization will go to a new bank and open an entirely new bank account in the nonprofit's name. They will then deposit checks that are sent to the nonprofit in that account, withdraw the funds and use the money for their own purposes.

2. Fraud - Someone will create a fake company that pretends to be a legitimate vendor of the nonprofit. They will provide fake invoices to the nonprofit and pay for fake services to the fake company.

3. Misappropriation of Funds - Someone with access will use the nonprofit's debit card for personal purchases.

Now that you know ways fraud commonly occurs in nonprofits, here are also a few things you can do to reduce the likelihood of financial scandals in your nonprofit:

1. Background checks - require that anyone that works for your nonprofit pass a background check. This will help you know if prospective employees have a criminal record or history of fraud.

2. Check references - Before you hire someone or allow them to get involved with your nonprofit, request references and call the references to inquire as to the person's character.

3. Check cash in the account - You should make it a habit of monitoring cash positions in your nonprofit's bank account regularly so that you can immediately report any suspicious activity.

4. Pay attention to vendors - When reviewing the bank account ledger, if you see any suspicious vendors that were paid from the charity's account - inquire and make sure they are legitimate.

5. Accounting Software - Use actual software to monitor financial transactions within your nonprofit so that you can recognize trends and monitor financial activity.

6. Limit cash - Try not to accept cash to the best of your ability. Instead, try to process payments via debit or credit cards since electronic payments are easier to track

7. Financial Controls - Require that checks are signed by multiple people within your charity for accountability purposes.

8. Lock up checks - Do not leave the nonprofit's checkbook out in the open as an easy target for theft.

9. Check work during vacations - Encourage your staff and employees to go on vacations. When they are out of the office, take this opportunity to check their desk, computer, email and any electronic records they may have. Make sure you have provided them with an email policy in advance letting them know that emails are the property of the company and that they should not assume any expectation of privacy when using company equipment or devices.

10. Be honest - Don't embellish accomplishments of your nonprofit or overstate expenses.

11. Segregate duties - Make sure different members of your staff are handling different financial tasks within your charity so that there is accountability and no one person has complete access to everything. Your CPA or accountant can help you with properly dividing up the roles.

12. Dissolution - If you decided to shut down your nonprofit, make sure that all assets (cash, equipment, property, etc.) are transferred to another tax-exempt nonprofit per the I.R.S. Code instead of going into the wallets of a board member or stakeholder.

What are Financial Statements

Every day, your nonprofit is accepting donations and spending money toward your mission. Instead of having to spend hours poring over hundreds or thousands of individual transactions (purchases and deposits) on the bank statements of your nonprofit account and doing the math to reach conclusions, you should generate financial statements for the nonprofit.

Financial statements are scorecards that let you view the health of a nonprofit by looking at a summary of its transactions or activities on a few pages. They are far less cumbersome than having to review hundreds of receipts and pages of bank statements. Financial statements are generated using a commonly accepted set of accounting principles or rules that allow nonprofit founders, board members, banks, and funding organizations to compare nonprofits from different industries in a universal way.

Financial statements are similar to sheet music for musicians. They allow people that are unfamiliar with a song, or in this case your nonprofit, to read the sheet music (financial statements) and immediately understand the music (the health of your nonprofit).

Why Financial Statements Are Important

Even though you are keeping your own records and tracking numbers for your nonprofit, it may be a good idea to generate financial statements on a regular basis.

Financial statements can help your nonprofit in the following ways:

1. Know the health of your nonprofit. Financial statements allow you to easily track many of the numbers that are important to know if your nonprofit is healthy and growing.

2. Know if your nonprofit is in the "black". Financial statements will allow you to see all of your expenses and your income on one page (typically). This will let you know immediately if you are making money or losing money in your nonprofit. For example, you will be able to see if the donations you receive from events are more than the donations you receive from online campaigns, etc. You can also tell if you're spending too much on staff, programming, or if you need to increase the budget in those areas.

3. Allows Others to Understand Your Nonprofit. In the future, you may decide that you would like to apply for grants or apply for a bank loan. In each of these scenarios, you will likely need to have financial statements prepared for your nonprofit so that the other parties (lenders, funding sources, etc.) can assess the financial health of your nonprofit.

3 Types of Financial Statements

There are three (3) primary types of financial statements: Income Statement (also known as the Profit & Loss Statement), Balance Sheet and Statement of Cash Flows. It would take an entire book to discuss how powerful each of these financial statements is and explain all of the ways that they can benefit your nonprofit. However, here is a brief overview of each statement:

1. Income Statement / Profit & Loss Statement (P&L) – On the most basic level, the Income Statement tells you how much money your nonprofit brought in and the bills the nonprofit had during a certain period of time. In order to make money in a nonprofit, you will need to have money left over after you pay all of your bills. This is a basic definition of "profit". The P&L lets you see the "bottom line" or your profit or loss after everything was paid during a specific time period (month, quarter, year, etc.) Here are just a few things an income statement will tell you about your nonprofit:

• How well is your nonprofit performing

• Is your nonprofit profitable (making money after the bills are paid)?

• Are you over budget or paying too much in some areas?

2. Balance Sheet – The Balance Sheet lets you see your assets (things you own) and your liabilities (what you owe others) at any given moment in your nonprofit. Examples of assets would be cash in your bank account, all equipment your nonprofit owns and accounts receivable (money other people owe you). Examples of liabilities would be credit card debt, and loans and wages owed to employees. Here are just a few of the things a balance sheet will let you know about your nonprofit:

- If you need more cash reserves (money saved)
- If you can handle more debt
- If you can handle growing or expanding
- If you need to be more aggressive with collecting money owed to you

3. Statement of Cash Flows – To put it simply, a Statement of Cash Flows tells you where your money is coming from and how it is being spent during a period of time. Some nonprofits are profitable but go out of business because they did not have enough "cash on hand" to pay their bills. This can happen if the timing of when your bills are due and when you get paid is not aligned. Your Statement of Cash Flows can help you see if this is or will be a problem and correct it in advance.

Here are a few things you can learn about your nonprofit from reviewing your Statement of Cash Flows:

- How much are you bringing in from sales and day-to-day nonprofit operations?
- How much money did you use to buy equipment or other assets?
- How much money did you borrow?
- Are you bringing in enough cash to pay your bills?

How to Create Financial Statements

Again, financial statements are a powerful tool for managing the performance of your nonprofit. Here are a few ways that you can create financial statements to increase the effectiveness of your nonprofit operations:

1. Do it Yourself. You can buy software or an app for your cell phone or tablet or you can use a cloud-based financial management website to manage your money and create financial statements. You can also create them using Microsoft Excel templates. Although it may take you some time to understand everything when you first start, taking the time to learn how to read and understand these financial statements will make you a savvier nonprofit founder, board member, officer or volunteer. Understanding financial statements will also help you communicate with others about your nonprofit. Consider visiting Lynda.com for online classes and tutorials regarding understanding and creating financial statements.

2. Hire a Bookkeeper or Accountant. Consider hiring a bookkeeper or accountant to prepare financial statements for your nonprofit.

Keep in mind, it's never too late to begin using these powerful financial tools as you run your nonprofit. Now that we understand ways you can avoid financial fraud and the importance of reviewing the financials of your nonprofit regularly, let's talk how to avoid I.R.S. trouble when recruiting volunteers.

Chapter Fifteen

Chapter 13: How to Avoid I.R.S. Trouble When Recruiting Volunteers

*W*hen I first started my nonprofit, I did almost everything by myself. We would host large leadership conferences for students and I would negotiate and book the venues, handle student recruitment and registration, raise money for the event, book the speakers, design the marketing collateral and more!

Until one year, I was so utterly exhausted that I realized that I wasn't able to even enjoy the event or appreciate the lives that we were changing. That is when I realized I needed to learn how to do things differently.

I started creating systems and processes to document and create procedures for the tasks I was doing. This allowed me to delegate to others without sacrificing quality since the procedures allowed them to execute the tasks exactly the way I would have. I even created *"decision trees" to allow them to analyze and make decisions the same way I would. This allowed us to be able to grow and handle more of everything because it was no longer all falling on me. My law firm helps clients create similar systems for their nonprofits. However, there is still a lot of liability involved with building a volunteer team. Here are some things you can do to protect yourself and your charity.*

An important part of starting your 501c3 nonprofit will be assembling a team of volunteers to help you execute your vision. Volunteers can be a huge benefit because they provide you with a team that can carry out various projects and initiatives. This allows you to be more effective since you can then focus on other aspects of your nonprofit while having skilled individuals get things done on your behalf.

As with most blessings, they can also be a curse if you are not careful in the way that you structure the volunteer opportunity. You need a **Volunteer Agreement** to help you to minimize the risk of the most common types of liability associated with building a team. My law firm prepares Volunteer Agreements for clients all of the time to help them build smart volunteer programs that avoid lawsuits.

Here are just a few of the clauses that you will want to be included within your agreement to make sure you and your nonprofit are legally protected:

1. The volunteer needs to acknowledge that they're agreeing to donate their services to your nonprofit;

2. The volunteer should acknowledge that they are not expecting and waive their right to any present or future payment (salary, wages, or other benefits) for the work they do for the nonprofit;

3. The volunteer needs to be willing to complete any required

training and follow the rules of the nonprofit;

4. The volunteer will need to acknowledge that they are not an employee of the nonprofit;

5. The volunteer should acknowledge that they will be held personally liable for any damages they cause to third parties for anything they do outside of their volunteer work;

6. The volunteer should acknowledge that they will be held personally liable for any damages they cause to third parties during their volunteer work if they were negligent;

7. The volunteer should agree to confidentiality and non-disclosure terms about sensitive and confidential nonprofit information;

8. The volunteer should agree that any work performed (e.g., presentations, etc.) while volunteering for the nonprofit becomes the property of the nonprofit;

9. And more!

If you make sure that you have a signed Volunteer Agreement on file for each of your volunteers, you will at least reduce the risk of some of the primary lawsuits and legal actions that take place when you have volunteers on your team.

Now that we have discussed how to avoid liability when bringing volunteers into your nonprofit organization, let's talk about how to legally pay yourself and others a salary.

Chapter Sixteen

Chapter 14: How to Avoid I.R.S. Trouble When Paying Yourself

*N*ot everyone is interested in being paid a salary from their nonprofit. I personally have never been paid for any of the work I've done for Revolution Leadership, and I do not have any plans of asking for anything in the foreseeable future. To me, the work that I do is simply my way of giving back and I am fortunate to have other sources of income to support myself financially.

However, if it is your desire to be paid from your nonprofit - there is nothing wrong with that either! Running a nonprofit takes both time and effort - both of which deserve compensation if you so choose. In this chapter, I will share how you can pay yourself and others the right way.

Can nonprofit founders and get paid for working for a nonprofit?

One of the most common misconceptions when it comes to nonprofits is that nonprofit founders are not allowed to be paid if they work for their own nonprofit. That is absolutely untrue! There are hundreds of thousands of nonprofits throughout the United States that employ individuals that work for them on a full-time basis. This is perfectly legal because our government realizes that it would be very difficult to ask people to do the work needed to grow a charity without any form of compensation.

Can board members get paid for working for a nonprofit?

Can board members be paid for their work with a nonprofit? It is commonly held that board members should not be paid for their work for a nonprofit. Unlike for-profit companies whose board members are often handsomely paid, nonprofit board members are seen as volunteering their services. Since they are viewed as public servants, it is seen as inappropriate for them to be paid. However, they can be reimbursed for reasonable out-of-pocket expenses that are related to their service for the board. These expenses can include but aren't limited to, mileage, meals, parking, and more.

I always recommend that nonprofits create a written Expense Reimbursement Policy for board members. My firm drafts this for nonprofit organizations. Basically, this is a written policy that lists clear rules to regulate when and how board members can be reimbursed for their expenses so that nonprofits are open and honest as it relates to this policy. In some states, if board members are paid, this can make them no longer qualify for the immunity that some states offer volunteer board members when it comes to lawsuits.

How much can you legally pay yourself?

Now that we understand that it is perfectly legal for nonprofit founders and officers to get paid a salary for the work that they do for the nonprofit, let's talk about how much you can be paid.

How much you can be paid is called "Executive Compensation." The rules for how much you can get paid from a nonprofit are based on the rebuttable presumption test of Section 4958 of the Internal Revenue Code and Treasury Regulations Section 53.495 8-6. Here is what it says in layman's terms. A nonprofit cannot pay you more than what is reasonable for the services you have performed.

So how do you know if what you want to be paid is considered reasonable? Your nonprofit will need to form an Executive Compensation Committee (we'll talk about this more in a moment) and they will need to research the market and get data to help them decide on what a reasonable amount should be. Here are the steps to do this legally:

1. Appoint a Committee. The board of directors of the nonprofit should appoint a Compensation Committee. Here is an example of reasonable criteria for the committee members:

a. The individuals serving on the committee that will help determine the amount that key employees of the nonprofit are paid should be knowledgeable as it relates to the area of executive compensation (e.g., managers, background in human resources, etc.)

b. The committee members should not be in a position where they will financially benefit from the result.

c. The committee members should not be paid by the nonprofit.

d. The committee members should not have a close relationship with the person whose salary they will be determining.

2. Conduct a Survey. The Compensation Committee will want to do a market survey of nonprofits to determine average salaries for similar positions.

a. The committee will need to find other nonprofits that offer similar programs, are located in similar locations, have similar numbers of employees and have similar gross revenue.

b. The committee will also need to take into consideration how much the nonprofit can actually afford to pay.

c. The compensation of key personnel and staff should not be the majority of the nonprofit's budget or donors may not feel that enough of the funding is going toward the actual programs.

d. The data needs to be documented so that if the I.R.S. ever audits the nonprofit – there is a paper trail to substantiate the reasons for the salary amounts chosen by the committee.

e. The committee members can confer with experts in human resources or similar consultants to make sure that their conclusions are reasonable.

f. The committee can also hire a third party to compare compensation data from similar nonprofit organizations and prepare a report for their consideration.

3. Make a Recommendation. The compensation committee will then recommend a Compensation Package to the Board of Directors for approval.

a. This Compensation Package will include a salary level for the position based on the findings from the research.

b. Meeting minutes should document the attendees of the committee, data evaluated, how the findings were analyzed and the actual recommendations.

4. Vote on the Recommendation. The entire board of directors will need to vote to approve the package.

a. There has to be "transparency" in the process. Meaning, all board members should then be allowed to vote on the adoption of the package

b. A meeting should be called

c. There must be quorum as defined by the nonprofit Bylaws

d. Written meeting minutes should be taken to document the meeting

e. A resolution should be written and adopted affirming the decision of the board

How to legally go about paying yourself and others?

Once the board has established how much you can be paid, the board will need the employees to do the following:

1. Sign an Employment Agreement – This should list ALL of the ways that the employee is being paid;

2. If the staff person is not a part-time or full-time employee, an Independent Contractor Agreement should be signed;

3. Hire an accountant to set up payroll, tax withholdings, etc;

4. Run payroll and pay the person as agreed;

5. Provide them with a W-2 Statement for their taxes or a Form 1099 if they earned over $600 as an independent contractor;

The easiest way to calculate payroll taxes for employees

My law firm uses a company called Gusto to process our payroll. Before I began hiring full-time employees, I was always worried about the paperwork that would be involved and feared miscalculating the tax withholdings. Gusto eliminates this problem! It is a simple to use online platform that does all of the math for you! You are able to add how much you want to pay your employees (by the hour, salary, etc.) and it will calculate all of the withholdings for you. The best part is that it also handles all of the reporting and filings to your state and federal authorities. I have had many colleagues that used expensive payroll companies that had fees for every filing. Gusto is a simple flat fee each month and I've never had any issues with them. (No, I'm not sponsored by them and they did not pay me to say this).

If you're interested in giving them a try, I've included my affiliate link in the resources section of the book. It gives you a chance to try them out for 2 months for free and gives me a gift card for introducing you to them.

What happens if you don't follow the I.R.S. executive compensation guidelines?

Keep in mind that the penalties for not following the I.R.S. guidelines regarding executive compensation can be severe. The I.R.S. legally conducts "Compliance Checks" for nonprofits to make sure that they are following these guidelines. If not, they can legally impose penalties of up to 200% of the "excess benefit" or the amount that an employee of the nonprofit was overpaid or excessively compensated for the services they gave the nonprofit for each transaction. Typically, the person that receives the payment (e.g., the employee) is the one that gets the penalty so don't allow a charity to pay you more than what is reasonable based on actual research.

Now that we understand the guidelines for getting paid for working for a nonprofit, let's talk about how to avoid liability when making decisions for your nonprofit.

Chapter 15: How to Avoid Liability When Making Decisions for Your Nonprofit

*S*tarting and running a 501c3 nonprofit requires you to make decisions. You'll need to make personnel decisions as it relates to recruiting volunteers and hiring staff. You may be involved with decisions as a board member. You'll have to make decisions as you are hosting community programs and fundraisers. There will be financial decisions to be made regarding how to spend funds as well as how to finance major purchases. If you want to avoid legal trouble as well as trouble with the I.R.S., you will need to have a plan of action as to how you will make decisions in a way that is in compliance with the law.

The way you make decisions matters because your actions no longer affect just you. As a nonprofit founder, director, committee member, employee, volunteer or supporter, you're accountable to the government (e. g., state and federal government), the people that work with you (your board members, committee members, etc.), people that rely on you (e. g., members of the community that utilize your services) as well as the people that support you (your donors, funding sources, sponsors, etc.).

Here are some recommendations for ways to avoid legal trouble as you are making decisions for your nonprofit:

1. Vote on Major Decisions.

If the nonprofit has a major decision to be made, you want to make sure that you give the board of directors an opportunity to vote on the decision. This makes it clear that you did not act unilaterally if the decision ends up not working out. Instead, it shows that you followed protocol by bringing the opportunity to the board and giving them a chance to weigh in and vote to either support or reject the decision.

2. Document Decisions with Resolutions.

The next thing you will want to do is to record the votes in writing. You will want to document or record any major company actions by writing meeting minutes that summarize who attend the meeting, what took place and the outcome of any votes on issues. Next, you will want to create a resolution on behalf of the nonprofit "ratifying" or formally accepting the decision. It is important to have these things documented so that your board of directors do not later have "amnesia" and no longer recall that they all played a role in determining the course of action of the charity - even if it is a failed one.

How to Keep Records that Meet I.R.S.

Standards

Once you have voted on and documented the decisions that have been made on behalf of your nonprofit, you will need to make sure that you keep proper financial records, nonprofit records, and tax records to remain in compliance with the law.

There are several key documents that you want to have accessible at all times as it relates to your nonprofit. These documents are the foundation of good record keeping as it relates to running a nonprofit. Here are a few of the main documents that you need to keep in a safe place in order to protect yourself as well as your nonprofit:

Legal Records

1. Articles of Incorporation

This is the formal charter document for your nonprofit that is filed with your state. It should be prepared with asset protection clauses, limited liability clauses as well as the language that the I.R.S. and major grants require.

2. Federal Employer Identification Number (FEIN)

The FEIN or taxpayer identification number is like a social security number for your nonprofit. This number allows donations that are given to your nonprofit to be viewed separately from personal income you receive that you have to report on your personal taxes.

3. Application for Tax-Exemption

This is the actual application you filed with the I.R.S. (or that your nonprofit attorney filed on your behalf) to obtain tax-exempt status. You will need to keep a copy of this on file as well as any addendum you submitted or letters received from the I.R.S.

<u>4. I.R.S. Determination Letter (Tax exemption Letter)</u>

This is the letter the I.R.S. provides you with once your nonprofit is approved stating that you officially have tax-exempt status. You will need to keep this on file as most grants and funding opportunities require a copy of it.

<u>5. Bylaws</u>

These are the governing rules for your nonprofit. You will need to make sure the most recently adopted version of the Bylaws is on file and signed by the appropriate board members.

<u>6. Meeting Minutes</u>

Meeting minutes serve as a transcript that documents what took place during the official meetings you have with your board and committee members for your nonprofit.

<u>7. Letters & Correspondence from the I.R.S.</u>

If you ever send or receive a letter from the I.R.S., make sure you keep a copy in your business records.

<u>8. Nonprofit tax returns</u>

Make sure the Form 990s that you have filed for at least the last 3 years (or as many as you have if you are a new nonprofit) are kept in your Corporate Minute Book.

<u>9. Resolutions</u>

They document key votes and decisions that were made and formally adopted by your nonprofit.

Asset Records

As your nonprofit grows, you may acquire assets. Assets include things of value such as property, equipment, automobiles, etc. that are titled in the name of the nonprofit. As with financial records, you will want to keep the original (whenever possible) and/or a copy of everything that relates to the asset for your records. Here are some examples of the documents that you should be keeping as records for the assets belonging to your nonprofit:

1. Bill of Sale, Receipts, Assignments or Transfer Documents

2. Deeds and Title documents

3. Proof of Insurance (e.g., Directors & Officers Insurance) and Policies

4. Closing documents

5. Loans, Notes or Mortgages

Human Resources & Vendor Records

As your nonprofit hires people, you will want to keep accurate and complete records of their employment. Here are some examples of the documents that should be kept as records of the employees and vendors of your nonprofit:

1. Employment Agreements;

2. Background check records;

3. I-9 Forms;

4. Independent Contractor Agreements;

5. Personnel files;

6. Timesheets;

7. Wages, taxes withheld, resolutions approving wages, and industry research

8. Substantiating rates;

9. Vendor Contracts;

10. Bids; Proof of compliance with conflict of interest policies;

11. 1099-MISC tax forms for fees paid to independent contractors;

Financial Records

When it comes to financial records, the general rule is to keep a copy of everything that relates to money that comes into the nonprofit as well as money that leaves the nonprofit. Here are some examples of the documents that you should be keeping as records for your nonprofit:

1. Nonprofit bank account statements. Keeping your bank account statements is important because your bookkeeper may need them when preparing your financials. You may also need them in order to get a loan for the nonprofit in the future.

Here are a few guidelines for managing your nonprofit bank account:

• Have a separate bank account for your nonprofit.

• Do not buy personal items using your nonprofit account. This is called co-mingling. Instead, write yourself a salary check from your nonprofit account (based on the executive compensation rules we discuss in this book), deposit it into your personal account and then pay the personal bill out of your personal bank account.

• Check your bank statements (called "reconciling") each month to make sure the balances are correct and that you have not been charged for bank fees or fees you did not approve.

2. Nonprofit Bank Account Deposit Slips.

Particularly if you accept cash, you should make copies or download your deposit slips from your bank's website as evidence that the funds were deposited. This is important because if you are ever audited by the I.R.S., you may need these records to prove the income you received.

3. Copies of checks received.

Keep records of the money you are paid.

This is important because the I.R.S. may require that you prove the income you listed on your nonprofit's annual tax return.

4. Canceled checks.

These are checks that you have written to other people to pay bills that have already cleared or been deposited. Keep a copy of them for your records to prove that you have paid your vendors. Canceled checks also prove that you paid for nonprofit expenses that you are deducting.

5. Receipts from purchases.

Receipts prove that the funds you spent from your nonprofit account were used for legitimate tax-deductible nonprofit expenses. Keeping copies of receipts from nonprofit purchases allows you to be prepared in case the I.R.S. audits you and asks you to provide evidence of the money you spent for your nonprofit.

6. Nonprofit credit card statements (if you have any)

7. Any invoices that you have submitted to vendors.

This shows payments that vendors owe you and allows you to keep track of the money you should be receiving.

8. Budget

Budgets allow you to plan for how you will spend donations that the nonprofit receives. You should keep records of this information so that you can compare past years with future years to monitor your growth.

9. Contracts.

Anytime you agree to hire someone (e.g., attorney, accountant, event planner, graphic designer) or you agree to perform a service for someone (e. g., speak at an event, plan a conference, etc.) you need a contract in writing. This ensures that both parties understand the terms (how much they will be paid, when the work is due, who owns the rights) and protects you if you ever need to sue them for not performing. You should always keep a copy of the contract signed by both parties but at the minimum signed by the other party.

Corporate Minute Book

One of the best ways to keep track of all of your nonprofit records and important legal documents is to invest in a Corporate Minute Book. A Corporate Minute Book is an elegant, custom-made portfolio with your nonprofit name engraved, that is specifically designed to keep all of your important nonprofit legal documents.

Corporate Minute Books often include actual nonprofit seals that you can use to signify that a document is an official document of your nonprofit.

Corporate Minute Books often include ledgers to document donations and expenses.

You will want to keep the signed originals of the various documents referenced in this chapter in your Corporate Minute Book for easy reference and access if and when needed.

You should, of course, keep digital or scanned copies of these key documents as a backup. You can save them on an external hard drive as well as maintain a cloud-based copy in the event that something happens to your originals.

My law firm offers Corporate Minute Books for purchase by our clients as well as provide a Digital Minute Book which allows bank-grade level security cloud-based storage for key documents for safekeeping. If you would like to order one, feel free to contact our law firm or any vendor that offers them.

Do you have to show people your financials or other records when asked?

A question I am often asked by nonprofits is "Do you have to show people your financials or other nonprofit records when asked?" **The Public Disclosure Rule** is a rule promulgated by the I.R.S. that tells you when you need to share your nonprofit's information with someone that asks from the general public. The rules say that when someone asks, tax-exempt organizations must make certain documents available to the public for inspection. Here are the documents that you have to make available:

1. Application for Tax-exemption
2. I.R.S. Determination letter
3. Last 3 filed nonprofit annual returns

You can only charge the person that asks to see the records for copies – but you cannot charge them for the right to inspect. You don't have to provide the actual information that you used to prepare the documents, just the documents you filed.

Now that we've covered how to make decisions for your nonprofit as well as the types of records you should keep to stay in compliance, how to avoid losing your entire nonprofit by keeping up with annual filings.

Chapter Eighteen

Chapter 16: How to Avoid Losing Your Entire Nonprofit by Keeping up with Annual Filings

*I*n 2011, the I.R.S. announced that it had revoked the tax-exempt status of over 275,000 nonprofits due to failure to file an annual return in compliance with the Pension Protection Act (PPA) of 2006. This Act changed the reporting requirements for small nonprofits and gave the I.R.S. the right to automatically take away a nonprofit's tax-exempt status if it did not file for three consecutive years - even if they were a small organization with minimal revenue. Unfortunately, Revolution Leadership was one of those organizations.

I applied for tax-exempt status for Revolution Leadership before I was an attorney. I was still in my early twenties and asked someone

I thought was knowledgeable if we needed to file any annual returns since we were a small nonprofit at the time and did not have much income. They told me "no" and I believed them. Because I relied on someone that was not a nonprofit attorney and was unaware that the law had changed - my nonprofit lost our tax-exempt status that year.

I had to spend time and money going through the arduous process of reapplying and learning the new requirements. Learn from my mistake. Stay on top of nonprofit laws yourself - or work with a knowledgeable nonprofit attorney that stays on top of the ever-changing requirements for you so that you do not find yourself in the same situation.

An important part of running or managing a nonprofit is making sure that you are current with your annual filings. Although you can hire someone to handle it for you, it is always good to at least understand the basics of what you will be responsible for filing so that you can make sure that your nonprofit is still in good standing with the I.R.S.

Here are some of the main forms that you should expect to file for your nonprofit. Please be advised that I am not an accountant or CPA so you will need to check with your own accountant or tax specialist to make sure that these specific forms apply to your individual situation. The purpose of this chapter is to give you a point of reference regarding potential questions to ask and potential forms you can expect to complete for your nonprofit.

Federal Filings

On the federal level, the most important thing to remember is that every year you will be responsible for filing an annual nonprofit tax return with the I.R.S. This return is called the Form 990 Annual Exempt Organization Tax Return (Federal). Here are a few important specifics regarding this form:

Form 990 Annual Exempt Organization Tax Return (Federal)

• Churches and religious organizations are exempt from this requirement

• Must be filed by the 15th day of the 5th month after the end of your organization's accounting period (May 15th)

• If you do not file it for 3 years in a row, they can take away your tax-exempt status

Form 990-T Unrelated Business Income

If your nonprofit is earning income that has nothing to do with your exempt purposes, you have to pay taxes on that income just like other businesses if it is $1,000 or more. If this is the case, you are required to file a Form 990-T with the I.R.S.

State Filings

On the state level, every year you will need to file a few things depending on the requirements of your individual state: Here are a few important specifics:

1. Annual Report

This is typically the filing you will need to submit to your state's Division of Corporations. The purpose of an annual report is to renew your nonprofit registration with the State. Some states charge a substantial late fee if it is filed after the deadline (In Florida, a $400 late fee is charged if filed after May 1st each year).

2. State tax exemption

In addition to your federal tax-exempt status, some states require that you apply for a state-level tax-exemption. There typically is no fee to apply but it may need to be renewed annually depending on your state.

3. Fundraising Registration

All nonprofits that want to ask for donations will need to register in the states that they plan to "solicit" for donations.

Unfortunately, there isn't a national registry, so you have to register in each state individually.

In sum, these are the primary annual filings that you will need to submit each year. My law firm offers an annual membership to clients where we handle the filings for them in a timely manner each year. As long as you find a system that works for you, you will be able to keep your nonprofit active and avoid any I.R.S. penalties for failure to file.

Now that we've discussed the annual filings that you need to stay in compliance and stay out of trouble, let's discuss how you can avoid legal pitfalls by hiring a nonprofit attorney and how to find a good one.

Chapter Nineteen

Chapter 17: How to Avoid Legal Pitfalls by Hiring a Nonprofit Attorney

*W*hen I first started practicing law, I shared with an attorney that I respect, that my goal was to maintain a 100% success rate for my filings for my nonprofit clients. I shared how I had invested in creating a system to make sure my clients received the best outcome every time. To my consternation, he responded, "If you do it right the first time, they won't have a reason to hire you again." I was so disappointed to hear someone I respected infer that I needed to intentionally mess up client's work in order to make more money. I rejected that premise then and I still reject it today.

I believe that if you do excellent work, people will not only trust you and continue to work with you, they will tell other people about you and refer you more business. This has been the case the entire time I've been a practicing attorney. I share this to say that not all attorneys *are created equal. You deserve an attorney that will be committed to doing your work right - the first time around. Here is what you need to know to find a great nonprofit attorney.*

Why You Need a Legal Team

When you listen to interviews featuring successful people in the nonprofit industry, it is easy to be left feeling like they are just extraordinary people that were born with extraordinary talent and were able to climb to the top all by themselves. Although many successful people are very talented, the thing that most successful people in the nonprofit industry have in common is that they have a team behind them that contributes to their success.

For example, you may only see them hosting major fundraising events, being interviewed by the media, managing their staff and coordinating projects and major initiatives that make a difference in the community. Yet, many of the most notable nonprofit founders and executives have worked with the best nonprofit lawyers to structure their organization for growth and advise them on decisions that will lead to them achieving their goals. They work with accountants that make sure they keep accurate records of the money they raise and provide transparent reports to their donors. They employ office managers and personal assistants to help handle the day-to-day operations involved in running their nonprofit. They are rarely doing it alone – but instead are winning because they have the support of an extraordinarily talented team that helps them accomplish more and make fewer mistakes due to relying on their team's expertise.

The same thing applies to you. You may not be running a

nonprofit with a $1 million-dollar annual budget (yet) – but you still need to start building a team. You can try to navigate all of the different aspects of starting a successful nonprofit yourself – state legal paperwork, federal legal filings, fundraising registration, annual filings, board of director recruitment, volunteer recruitment, fundraising, programming, etc. If you do, you risk burning out or quite simply spending so much time trying to learn everything that you don't have enough time to do what you do best – focus on making a difference.

Modern technology allows us to handle more things ourselves. However, there is always a cost to doing things yourself – time. We are each only given a limited number of hours in the day. The most successful people use their hours doing what they do best. They build a team of people to help them in the other areas. This allows you to get more done since you are doing what you are good at instead of trying to become an expert at everything. It will also help you grow because you will be taking advantage of the experience of other professionals to move your nonprofit forward in all of the other areas. This means making fewer mistakes and getting results faster - because you can ask the experts on your team for guidance, best practices, and advice.

Since this entire book is about avoiding legal trouble and issues with the I.R.S., I'm going to share why the first member of your team should be an excellent nonprofit attorney and exactly how to find one.

What is a Nonprofit Attorney?

Believe it or not, there are different types of attorneys that specialize in different things. Just like there are doctors that specialize in helping children, women, focusing on hearts, ears, teeth, etc. - there are different types of lawyers that specialize in different things.

A nonprofit attorney is one that specializes in helping nonprofits. They handle preparing and filing the legal paperwork to start your nonprofit and make sure it is structured the right way and everything is done correctly. The best ones also advise you as you grow. For example, a good nonprofit attorney can also give you guidance to help you get maximum benefit from your board of directors, raise money to achieve your goals, recruit volunteers, hire staff, create systems and processes so that you can delegate more and get more done without sacrificing quality and manage the various aspects of your nonprofit so that you can grow and achieve your goals.

Let me be clear. Your nonprofit attorney wouldn't be the person that you go to if you are in a car accident, if you are arrested for a criminal offense or if you need assistance with filing immigration papers.

These legal matters all require different types of attorneys that specialize in those areas. You could, however, ask your nonprofit attorney for a referral if you ever needed help with anything else legal. Although my firm focuses on nonprofit law - we regularly give our clients referrals to other attorneys when it's something that we don't handle.

Why You Need a Nonprofit Attorney

Now that we know what a nonprofit attorney does, let's talk about why it may be a good idea for you to add one to your team. While you are starting and growing your nonprofit, it may be tempting to skip the step of finding a nonprofit attorney. You may have heard that attorneys are expensive. This fact alone can be discouraging. Perhaps, you may have had a bad experience with an attorney or you feel like you don't need one since you don't exactly know how an attorney could benefit you when starting and growing your nonprofit.

Here are the top reasons you could benefit from having a nonprofit attorney on your team:

1. Form Your Nonprofit - An experienced nonprofit attorney can do everything you need to start a successful 501c3 nonprofit. They can file all of the state and federal paperwork that you need to be in compliance and avoid legal trouble as well as trouble with the I.R.S.

2. Answer Your Questions - As you start your nonprofit and continue to grow, you are going to have questions. You will have questions about removing board members, changing your nonprofit's address, transferring property to your nonprofit, accepting donations from donors overseas, partnering with other nonprofits, raising money, hiring employees, paying yourself a salary, etc. Having a nonprofit attorney on your team that knows the answers, understands your goals and can give you guidance when you need it will help you avoid costly mistakes and reach your goals faster.

3. Give You Strategy to Grow - So what is the very first thing you should do once your 501c3 nonprofit is approved? How do you build a sustainable base of donors? How do you keep volunteers engaged? A good nonprofit attorney can give you a step-by-step plan of action to grow and achieve your goals in record time such as:

- Help you raise funds (donations) from donors to grow your nonprofit;
- Help you apply for grants (or refer you to a grant writer that can assist)
- Help you hire staff and employees;
- Help you manage your staff and board of directors;
- Help you recruit volunteers;
- Help you pay yourself and your staff a salary and benefits;
- Help you create systems and processes to delegate more while maintaining the same quality of work as if you had done the tasks yourself;
- Make sure your personal assets (bank accounts, property, etc.) are protected in the event that your nonprofit is sued;
- Help you buy or lease office space or accept land and property donated to your charity;
- Establish other charities or foundations to allow you to give back to the community;
- Help you dissolve your nonprofit or transfer leadership if you no longer desire to be involved;
- And more!

4. Protect Your Intellectual Property – Apply for federal trademarks so that you can own the names of signature programs and events for your nonprofit.

5. Review Your Contracts - A nonprofit attorney will review your contracts to make sure they say what you think they say. From basic contracts like hiring a web developer to build a custom website for your charity - to reviewing the commercial lease agreement for downtown office space for your organization - you need to have your legal documents reviewed before signing them. Why? Because most contracts are written in "Legalese." This means the words may have different meanings in the law than what you would commonly think they mean. This is sometimes designed to make sure that one party (usually the person who had the contract made) can benefit over the other party without them knowing it.

The way that you can protect yourself is by making sure you have your own lawyer read your contracts and tell you what they mean. Otherwise, you'll still be legally responsible for fulfilling the contract or facing the penalties of breaching (violating) the agreement once you sign the deal - even if you honestly thought it said something different.

True story, I have had several clients that have shown me contracts they were planning on signing and told me what they "thought" the contracts said. These were all very intelligent, educated and successful people. One contract said that my client would be giving away all of her rights to her literary work (when she thought she was just giving the publishing company permission to print her book promoting her nonprofit). One contract said my client would have to pay the equivalent of 10 years worth of monthly rent **up front** if they ever decided they no longer wanted to lease the building (when my client thought they would only lose their security deposit). And the list goes on! The point is to have your own lawyer review your contracts before you sign them!

6. Advise You Regarding Opportunities – Your nonprofit lawyer should be able to analyze any potential partnerships, sponsorships or opportunities you receive to tell you what is in the best interest of your nonprofit. This book does not cover everything. You need an attorney to review each specific opportunity to make sure that you are seeing both the pros and cons. As they say, the devil is in the details. The difference between a good deal and a bad deal is found in the terms and an experienced lawyer can help you make sure you have the best terms.

7. Negotiate Deals – Once you know what the terms are, your nonprofit lawyer will negotiate for you so that you do not jeopardize your industry relationships. Let your lawyer be the bad guy (or girl) – not you. Remember, lawyers, are governed by strict rules that require them to fight for the best interests of their client. Even if you speak to another party's attorney, they are biased because they are required by law to fight for the best interests of their client – which is the other party – not your nonprofit. If you have your own lawyer, your lawyer can ask for things on your behalf without you appearing to be ungrateful or difficult to work with. You can blame the negotiations on your lawyer while reaping the benefits of having contracts that result in more donations for your charity and protect your legal interests.

8. Save You Money on Your Taxes – Legal fees are tax-deductible, so you can typically deduct your legal fees on your taxes to save on your tax bill.

9. Help You Avoid Costly Mistakes – It's usually cheaper to have something reviewed than it is to fight in court. You will likely only spend a few hundred dollars having your agreement reviewed or having a legal consultation. However, most lawsuits start in the two-thousand-dollar range.

10. Peace of Mind Knowing that Things are Done The Right Way - Unless you've read the entire I.R.S. Code and stay current with the ever-changing state and federal laws on a regular basis - there may be a lot of things that you don't know about starting and running your nonprofit. These things could result in costly mistakes that you can easily avoid by having an experienced nonprofit attorney doing the work for you or at the least advising you before you make decisions.

How much do attorneys cost?

How much will you have to pay to hire a nonprofit attorney to form your 501c3 nonprofit for you? The answer is it depends. Different attorneys have different rates based on their success rate, experience and the benefits that are included in their packages.

At my firm, we offer flat-fee packages for our nonprofit legal services. This means that our clients pay one fee and all of the services that we list in our package are included for that one fee. This is different from some law firms that charge by the hour and bill you for every minute you spend on the phone with them or every minute they spend doing work for you.

We prefer the flat fee method because it gives us an incentive to work efficiently for our clients - instead of being rewarded with more legal fees for taking longer to get work done.

The best I can say is that at minimum - you will need to pay for filing fees (the fees that go to the government to process your paperwork) in addition to legal fees (the fee paid to the lawyer for spending time doing the work for you.

Filing fees alone on the state level are on average around $100 and filing fees on the federal level (again depending on which form(s) you're filing) are on average $600. That means you will need at least

$700 just to cover the filing fees alone.

You should then budget above that fee to cover the legal fees for the attorney doing the work for you.

What to Look For in a Good Lawyer

Everyone has a different opinion as far as what qualities a good lawyer should have. Here are just a few of my thoughts on the subject:

1. Experience. Make sure they have represented people with similar nonprofits like yours. This will ensure that they are able to get things done the right way the first time they file instead of experimenting with your organization and having to redo work.

2. Easy to talk to. If you feel uncomfortable, intimidated or as if the lawyer does not have time for you then this may not be the attorney for you. Your lawyer should speak using words that you can understand and should be easy to talk to.

3. Willing to answer questions. If your attorney seems offended by you asking questions, then they may not be the best person. Make sure they are open and willing to give you both sides of the situation as well as answer your questions to make sure you understand everything that is taking place.

4. Up front pricing. A good lawyer should have enough experience to be able to estimate with reasonable certainty how much various services will cost you.

5. Responsive. Make sure the firm takes the time to get back to you in a timely manner before you hire them – or else you may never be able to reach them after you've paid them. I can't tell you how many of my firm's clients choose us because they were calling other firms and their calls were never returned.

6. Reputation. It's also helpful if the lawyer has positive reviews from past clients that they have represented in the past.

How to Find a Good Lawyer

The best way to find a good lawyer is to get a referral from someone that has a good one. If you have friends that have a successful nonprofit, you can ask them if they can refer a good attorney.

Otherwise, you can always go online and search for "nonprofit lawyer in Chicago (insert your city)." You'll see more results than you can handle. Take your time and go through them. Try and get a feel for the different lawyers and call a few until you find one that you feel comfortable with.

Many people assume that online companies, consultants, accountants and attorneys that apply for 501c3 tax-exempt status for their clients all do the same thing – so they might as well hire the person that is the least expensive. This could not be farther from the truth!

Contrary to popular belief, not everyone that advertises that they will file your application for tax-exemption has the knowledge and expertise required to prepare an application that will be approved by the Internal Revenue Service (I.R.S.).

Questions to Ask A Nonprofit Attorney Before Hiring Them

Here are some questions you should ask anyone that you are considering hiring to complete your application for tax-exemption in order to protect yourself and avoid being cheated.

1. *What is your success rate?*

Unfortunately, some companies are in the business of getting your money but not getting you the result you paid for – which is a nonprofit that is approved for tax-exempt status. Make sure you ask the company that you are thinking about hiring what their actual success rate is when it comes to getting applications for tax-exemption *approved.*

Many companies advertise how many filings they have submitted but conveniently leave out the percentage of clients that they have successfully obtained 501c3 status for. Why does this matter? If a company advertises that they file thousands of applications for tax-exemption for clients – but they only have a 50% approval rate – or they say they do not know their approval rate, then there may be a good chance that your application will not be approved. This means that you may end up spending months waiting for the I.R.S to give you their ruling on the application only to find out that your application was denied. The worst part about this is that the filing fees that you paid to the I.R.S. are non-refundable. This means that if the company you hire was not capable of preparing your application in a manner that would be approved by the I.R.S. – you could end up having lost valuable time as well as money.

My law firm is very proud of that fact that we have a 100% success rate with our applications for 501c3 tax-exemption since 2010 (Disclaimer: Past results do not determine future outcomes). We use our proprietary **4-Step Total Nonprofit Formation™** process in order to put ourselves in the best position to deliver our clients the result they hired us to achieve – a 501c3 tax-exempt nonprofit.

2. Have any of your clients successfully obtained grants?

Once you have asked a company you are considering hiring about their success rate as it relates to obtaining 501c3 status for their clients, the next question you want to ask them to avoid being cheated is *"Have any of your clients successfully obtained grants?"*

Even if you are planning on funding your nonprofit yourself or have no interest in obtaining outside funding or grants, you still want to ask this question. Why? Because if their clients have been able to qualify for grants - this usually means that the nonprofits they are forming are properly structured and able to meet high levels of scrutiny. Federal and private grants have very specific requirements and typically will not write a check to an organization that was not established properly.

On the other hand, if you are someone that desires to obtain grants to fund your nonprofit, this question is paramount. If you will need funds to finance your charitable initiatives and do not desire to pay for the operating budget for your nonprofit out of your own pocket, you should want the option to obtain funding from foundations, government agencies and companies throughout the country that offer grants and corporate sponsorships as a way to support the efforts of your 501c3 tax-exempt nonprofit organizations.

In order for you to obtain grant funding to cover your full-time salary with your nonprofit, pay for office space, programs, supplies, additional staff, and any other reasonable expenses, you need to ensure that your application for tax-exempt status is structured in a way that meets the criteria of grants. There are things that grant committees require from your formation documentation. If this criterion is not met, you will not be eligible to apply for funding.

How do you know if the person you are considering hiring knows how to do this? Ask them one simple question: *"Have any of your clients successfully obtained grants?"*

You may be surprised by the answer.

At my law firm, we have clients that earn full-time salaries working for their nonprofits as well as clients that receive funding from grants. We have clients that have obtained grants and corporate sponsorships from Walmart®, Target®, ChickFilA®, Olive Garden®, Enterprise®, city governments, to name a few.

3. What is included in your service?

The next question you want to ask after you have determined a company's success rate as well as if any of their clients have obtained grants is "What is included in your service?" Despite advertising that their service is a flat fee, some companies will add on the following fees to their price:

1. Responses to the I.R.S. - Some companies will quote you a very inexpensive price to file your application for tax-exemption. The problem is that filing the application is only half of the process. The other half is responding to the I.R.S. The I.R.S. will review your application. They will scrutinize your application and may send an official letter identifying issues with your application that need clarifying or your application will be rejected. You must respond by their deadline or the I.R.S. has the right to deny your application (no refunds). Some law firms may charge up to $400/hour on top of the quoted "flat fee" in order to prepare and submit a response for you. You want a package that includes these filings at no additional charge.

2. Filing Fees – Many companies do not include the filing fees that must be submitted to the I.R.S. within their "flat fee" quotes. At the time of this printing, these fees range from around $275 - $600. You also have state filing fees to pay in addition to this amount.

3. *Legal Representation* – Many companies will bill at an hourly rate anytime you have a question and want to call or email your nonprofit attorney during the application process. This can get quite expensive and is charged in addition to the flat fee. At my firm, we want our clients to be able to speak with their attorney, so we do not charge for every phone call or email unless it is beyond the scope of the services we agreed to do.

4. *State Tax Exemption* - As I shared previously in the book, some states require that you apply for a state exemption even if you have been granted tax-exempt status from the federal government.

5. *Fundraising Registration* - As we discussed earlier in the book, some states require that you register before you can raise money for your nonprofit.

6. *Registered Federal Trademark* - Apply for a trademark to own your nonprofit's name, logo, slogan and the names of your signature programs.

7. *D.U.N.S. Registration* - This number is required to apply for certain federal grants.

8. *Founder's Protection Bylaws™ or Standard Bylaws* - You want a package that includes drafting Bylaws for you by an attorney that specializes in nonprofit law. You should be given the option to have standard bylaws prepared. Or, if you are concerned about being wrongfully removed from your nonprofit after you've built the organization and are perhaps earning a generous salary, then you may want to consider having bylaws prepared that protect your rights as the founder. I've created proprietary "Founders' Protection Bylaws" that prevent founders from being wrongfully removed from their organization while still being in compliance with the I.R.S. and public policy and we prepare these often for our clients.

9. Budget/Financials - You want a package the includes a budget template that you can use to operate your nonprofit as well as completes the financials section of your IRS application if it is required. The last thing you want is to have to hire a separate CPA or accountant to do those parts of your application because they were not included in your original package.

10. Corporate Meeting Minutes - As you are running your nonprofit, we recommend that you record everything that takes place during the board meetings of your nonprofit.

11. Conflict of Interest Policy and Resolution - The I.R.S. recommends that you have a policy in place that shows how your nonprofit will handle conflicts of interest as well as a resolution showing that your board voted to adopt the policy.

12. Financial Setup – You want to make sure that your nonprofit is ready to receive donations and manage its finances on day one. Ask if the vendor includes all of the things you need to maintain financial compliance including your Receipt, Contribution Statement, IRS-required language acknowledging that nothing of value was given in exchange for the donation, guidance to give your bookkeeper on how to handle certain donations, etc.

13. Management – Choosing your board members and giving them proper expectations is critical to your success. You want to make sure you will receive guidance on how to pick your board and how to define their roles and activities so that they are able to help you reach your goals. You will want to make sure that a Board of Directors handbook is included so that you can share your expectations with your Board so that everyone on your team is on the same page.

14. *Marketing* – After you've setup your nonprofit, you'll need an effective strategy for getting the word out about your organization so that you can get donations and community support. You'll want the vendor you hire to offer marketing support such as Facebook/Meta and LinkedIn page setup, text for your website, logo design, flyer and business cards creation and more.

15. *Human Resources* – You should have a package that gives you everything you need to pay yourself and your team a salary legally (if you desire) so that you are in compliance with the IRS.

16. *Program Assistant* – There is a lot that goes into running your nonprofit. Recruiting a volunteer to serve as your Program Assistant and handle all of the day-to-day tasks for your nonprofit is critical. We have a program that has successfully helped founders recruit qualified and talented individuals that work for free while enabling them to grow their organizations.

17. *Training* – You will want your vendor to provide you with training and education so that your first board meeting and kickoff programs run smoothly.

18. *Fundraising Event Training* – You'll want to make sure your package offers proven tools to allow you to run successful fundraisers for your nonprofit without trying to figure things out through trial and error.

19. *Grant Writing* – If you're not planning on self-funding your charity, you will want a package that will include training on how to properly write grants to win more funds for your cause or give you the opportunity to hire an experienced grant writer to write grants for you.

20. Expense Reimbursement – You should get a package that gives you the ability to be reimbursed for the cost of legal fees & reasonable out of pocket expenses related to the setup of your nonprofit.

21. Corporate Kit – Make sure they offer a physical binder customized with your nonprofit's information so that you can keep up with all of your important legal documents in compliance with the I.R.S.

22. Annual Maintenance – You don't want to invest in setting up your nonprofit only to lose your organization because you missed a deadline or critical filing. Instead, look for a package that handles all of your renewals so that you can focus on your organization.

At my law firm, we have flat fee packages that include all of the items listed above and more!

In addition to those items, here are a few more questions that you can ask to make sure you are making a good decision:

1. What is your firm's specialization? This will let you know if they actually focus on nonprofits - or if it is one of the many things they do. For us, nonprofit law is our largest practice area and we have expertise in this area of law. This means we are equipped to handle any issue that the I.R.S. presents as it relates to starting your 501c3 nonprofit.

2. How many nonprofit applications have you filed? This will give you an idea of how much experience they have in this practice area. We've helped clients worldwide - with reviews on Google, Avvo and all of the major sites to prove it - since we've been in business since 2010 with a 100% success rate*. (*Disclaimer: Past results do not determine future outcomes).

3. How long have you been practicing nonprofit law? Again, this question will let you know how much experience they have with matters similar to yours. We've been helping nonprofit clients successfully since 2010.

4. What percentage of those applications have been approved? This question allows you to estimate the level of risk you are assuming by choosing to work with their law firm. Our success rate is 100%.*

5. Have they represented clients doing the same thing that you are? This will let you know if they have experience specifically with forming the same type of nonprofit that you need. We have successfully formed nonprofits in almost every industry imaginable, so we bring a wealth of knowledge and expertise to the table for our clients.

6. Do they bill you hourly for every phone call and email you send? This lets you know how much access to your attorney you will have for any given price. Our packages are flat fees so our clients are not charged any additional fees to communicate with their attorney about their application during the filing process.

7. Are you a Martindale-Hubbell rated attorney? If so, what is your rating? Martindale Hubbell is an established company that allows lawyers in the industry to rate other lawyers based on their competency, etc. I am honored to have been awarded the "Preeminent AV rated attorney" designation which is the highest credential you can have).

8. Do you have any disciplinary history with the bar? This will let you know if any of their past clients have filed a grievance or bar charge against them for allegedly unethical behavior, etc. Since we opened our doors in 2010, our attorneys do not have any disciplinary history and enjoy positive reviews from past clients on Google, Facebook, Avvo, etc.

In conclusion, a qualified nonprofit attorney can be a tremendous benefit to you and your nonprofit. As long as you do your research and keep in mind the questions above, you will position yourself to identify an attorney that can help you avoid costly mistakes.

Chapter Twenty

Chapter 18: How to Afford Startup Costs For Your Nonprofit

H opefully, you're now able to see at least some of the benefits of adding a nonprofit attorney to your team. Now let's address the elephant in the room. How do you afford startup costs for your nonprofit, including hiring a nonprofit attorney, if you're interested in hiring one? I realize this may not be a concern for everyone - but just in case it is I'm going to share a real-life story with you and give you several ways to find money to get started.

Muhammad was a young man that graduated from college and knew he wanted to make a difference. He became a teacher and one day visited a poor neighborhood. He believed that if people in that community were given a small loan to help them buy supplies to start a trade or start a small business, they would pay back the money and improve their life. He decided to use his own money to lend $27 to a few poor women. They repaid the money with interest. Muhammad knew that he had discovered something powerful that could help a *lot of people.*

There was only one problem. He didn't have enough money to continue making loans.

He decided to apply for a bank loan. He was approved for a loan to help him further his charitable mission. He used the loan from the bank to start the Grameen Bank, a community development bank that offered small loans to impoverished individuals.

Muhammad worked hard toward fulfilling his purpose of helping others by offering funding through his social enterprise. He believed that giving poor people access to money to start a business was a critical step in helping them break the cycle of poverty and improve their lives.

By July 2007, his bank had helped over 7.4 million people and awarded over $6.38 billion in small loans which he called "microcredit". In 2006, Mohammad Yunus won a Nobel Peace Prize and his work and his charitable endeavors inspired other modern nonprofits such as Kiva to also make capital available to impoverished people.

What would have happened if Muhammad had refused to get a loan to pursue his purpose? What if he had said "I'm going to wait until I pay for this myself? How many years would it have taken him to get started? How many millions of people would have remained unserved while he waited years trying to save enough money to pay for everything himself using only his teacher salary?

I would never encourage anyone to take on unnecessary "consumer debt." It's hardly ever a good idea to take out loans for things like clothes, shoes, video games, Christmas gifts, vacations or other items that you have to repay if you cannot afford them.

But have you ever wondered why Apple), one of the largest

companies in the world, would take out $98 billion in debt when it has over $192 billion in cash on hand? Would you agree that one of the largest companies in the world worth over $2 trillion is run by smart people? Why would they do that?

It's because they understand something many of us were never taught. At least I wasn't. They understand the difference between "consumer debt" and "business investment."

Consumer debt is when you're using debt to buy things that don't make any money. That is what happens when you use a credit card to buy clothes or shoes. You've borrowed the money but owning the clothes or shoes most likely won't make you any money to pay off the credit card.

But using a credit card or getting a small loan to start a business or nonprofit that will make money is called an "investment". You're using the "debt" to allow you to quickly get the resources you need to start operations and then you can repay the money and then continue making a positive impact on your community.

For example, many of our most successful clients start off by paying for our services with a credit card. We get them setup legally and give them the support they need to start running their nonprofit organization. Within months, most are able to quickly pay off the credit card bill from initial donations from their board members, money they raise from their first fundraiser or funding they receive from a corporate sponsorship or even a startup grant. The remaining funds are used to pay salaries and cover expenses needed to support their mission.

I'm not here to convince you of anything so you should make the decision that feels right to you. Regardless of how you feel, just know that in order to have something you've never had, you may have to step out of your comfort zone and do something you've never done.

Here are 15 ways to get the funds you need to start your nonprofit - including several ways that don't include debt. The most important part is to take action and do something to get the funds you need so that you can start making an impact.

1. **Ask Your Board Members to Donate** - According to the 2012 Nonprofit Research Collaborative Study, the majority of nonprofits have a policy that requires board members to make an annual donation. The median donation amount was $1,000. This means that if you want to raise $3,000, you only need to get three (3) people to serve on your board and donate $1,000 each. Or, you can ask six (6) people to donate $500.

2. **Ask for a payment plan.** Many companies will let you get started for less than the full amount if you don't have it. Our law firm offers payment plans that can make it easier to get started. Instead of paying everything up front, you can break it up into smaller payments. This let's you get started for as little as $199/month depending on the package.

3. **Get a 0% interest credit card.** Many small business credit cards and personal credit cards will give you the first year at 0% interest. This means you can use the card to start your nonprofit - then have 12 months to pay it off and not pay any interest. Apply at your local bank or visit bankrate.com to shop around for the best rates nationally.

This allows you to have plenty of time to setup your nonprofit and raise enough money to payoff the credit card before the interest starts.

4. **Get a home equity loan or cash-out refinance.** If you own a home and have equity in it, you can apply through your bank to take a loan against the equity. Use the funds to start your nonprofit and then pay yourself back. Many banks offer access to these funds without any prepayment penalties so it won't cost you anything if you pay it off early.

5. **Borrow from your retirement account.** If you have a retirement account (e.g., 401K, etc.), you can request to take a loan against the balance. Be sure to contact your fund manager and know that some penalties may apply. Use the funds to start your nonprofit and then pay yourself back.

6. **Borrow from your savings.** You can give your nonprofit a loan by borrowing from your savings account and paying yourself back. The way to ensure that you repay yourself is to take out a secure personal loan from your bank. The bank will freeze the $3000 that you put into an account, give you a check for $3000 and then you will pay back the amount in monthly payments typically with minimal interest. This will help you have the discipline to repay the amount because it will be an actual bill – versus you simply telling yourself to do it which can easily become less of a priority in lieu of other

more pressing bills.

7. **Use your personal funds** - One option is to use your own personal funds or savings to pay for legal services. If you have the financial resources available, this can be a straightforward way to get the legal support you need. However, if you do not have the necessary funds on hand, there are other options you can consider.

8. **Get a personal bank loan.** Banks will loan small amounts ($5000 or less) at low interest rates and let you pay it back within 5 years. Give your bank a call and let them know that you would like to apply for a "personal loan." Make sure the monthly payments are comfortable for you.

9. **Get a personal line of credit.** This is an account that is fully funded by the bank that you can borrow from at any time. You are simply required to make minimum payments on the balance each month. Again, ask for 0% interest promotions and use the funds to start your nonprofit and then pay yourself back.

10. **Borrow from Friends or Family**. Most friends and family members are reluctant to loan money because it does not feel like a loan but feels as if they are giving it away and will never be repaid. In order to overcome this, you have to approach them in a professional manner. Reach out to the most successful family members or friends that you know. Let them know you would like to share with

them an opportunity that would involve them earning 5% interest on their money. I guarantee you that statement alone will get anyone's attention because right now banks are offering less than 1%. Before you feel that this is not possible, realize that 5% interest on $3,000 is only $150. When you meet with them for coffee or lunch, make small talk and then share your story about what led you to want to start your nonprofit. Let them know that all you need is $3,000 to get started. You can actually ask them for less than that because remember you yourself should be giving plus hopefully a few board members so perhaps you will only need $1,000 from them. Let them know that the only thing you are waiting on is to obtain your tax exempt status so that you can get more people to donate and that the money will be used to hire an attorney to complete the process for you. You can also inform them that as soon as the process is complete, you plan to begin receiving donations and you will pay them back first. You may also want to let them know that they don't have to take your word for it, but that you will provide them with a legal document that obligates you to pay them back $1,000 + 5% interest by the end of the year. Our office prepares loan documents for our nonprofit clients that get started with us free of charge. If your friends and family cannot afford to lend you the money, ask them if they know anyone that may be interested. Here is a sample script you can use.

11. *I wanted to know if you would be willing to loan me $1000*

to start my nonprofit. Now, I'm not asking you to do this for free. I'm willing to sign a legal loan document that legally obligates me to pay you back the full $1000 plus 5% interest (which is $50) after one year. I'm going to use the money to get the formal paperwork done to start my nonprofit. This will allow me to raise more money since we'll be a tax-exempt organization – and the very first donations that come in will be used to repay you. [Pause and wait for their response] If you're not able, do you happen to know anyone else that may be interested? Do you mind if I mention that you gave me their information? Thanks so much!

12. **Ask for a Raise.** If the job you work for doesn't already have a promotion plan for you, you don't have to wait for them to offer a raise. You can ask for one. Research online to find out what other companies are paying people in your position. Read a few articles online about "how to ask for a raise" and make your pitch. Warning: Make sure you have been an ideal employee for at least a few months before doing this. You should be arriving early, staying late and completing all of your tasks with a good attitude and with excellence!

13. **Work Overtime.** Ask your employer if you can work extra hours for a limited amount of time in order to raise the funds.

14. **Apply for a different position within the company.** Most companies have other job openings within the company. Ask HR and apply for higher paying positions

within the company. If you don't get the job, don't be discouraged. Keep applying. It's a numbers game. The more positions you apply for - the greater your chances. You'll need to at least try for 10. Ask for feedback and make sure you fit the criteria of an ideal employee listed in tip #1.

15. **Sell Something.** Sign up for a free seller account on Facebook marketplace or Amazon. Both websites will let you sell household items that you're no longer using that may still have market value. Old cell phones, laptops, tablets, books, bicycles, video game consoles, musical instruments, etc. may give you the funding you need.

16. **Start a part-time business.** You can use your gifts and talents to raise funds to start your nonprofit. If you already make money on the side as a musician, selling baked goods, reviewing friend's resumes, etc., find a way to do more of it to make more money. You can do more by (1) getting more customers or (2) raising your prices. If you don't have as many customers as you want - it means you need to talk about what you do more. Use social media to talk about your successes and make sure all of your friends and family know exactly what you do and how good at it you are. The more you post and/or promote yourself - the more likely people are to remember you when they need something. So start talking about what you do more! If you're not currently selling your services, ask your friends or family what are

the top 3 things you're good at and consider starting a small business using those gifts and talents.

Once you've raised the money to get started, you're ready to reach out to a nonprofit lawyer for help. Here are a few things to keep in mind:

1. Free consultations. Many nonprofit lawyers and law firms will offer a free consultation in which they will listen to your situation and outline the steps they would take to assist you as well as give you a quote for their legal services. A few things to keep in mind as it relates to free consultations:

o Please know that just because the attorney represents nonprofits - this does not mean their services are free.

o Although the initial consultation is free - you should only schedule this consultation if you are (1) seriously considering moving forward with your nonprofit and (2) have a budget (or access to finances via a credit card, business partner, loan, tax refund, etc.) to pay for the legal service.

o For example, if the filing fees for your service are estimated at $700, you would at least want to have this amount available in addition to a job or some form of income that you could use to cover the legal fee before you schedule a free consultation.

o Some firms, including my own, may offer incentives during the free consultation if you sign up for a package within a certain time frame. Having funds readily available puts you in the best position to get the best deal for your nonprofit.

o Make sure you ask if they are willing to charge a flat fee (one-time fee) for their services instead of billing you by the hour (which can end up being far more expensive).

2. Legal Consultation. If you just want to ask questions and do the work yourself, hiring a nonprofit attorney for only a legal consultation may be a good option for you. A legal consultation can cost you anywhere from $350-$450 depending on the attorney, their credentials and the nature of what you want to discuss. Please keep in mind though that for most of our services - due to their complexity - it is always far less expensive for our clients to hire us for a package (which usually include unlimited access to us for questions plus us doing all of the work) instead of just doing the consultation. The choice is yours. Make sure you have your specific questions written down in advance before you meet or call your attorney so that you can take advantage of the time you have with them. Some lawyers will even let you email your questions in advance - which means they will be able to answer them more efficiently.

3. Share Competing Offers - If there is a law firm you want to work with, but you feel like you've found another company that appears to offer more value for a better price, give the original firm the opportunity to compete. At my firm, we know that there isn't anyone that will work harder and fight harder for clients than we will. As such, we encourage anyone to do us the courtesy of allowing us the opportunity to match a competing offer they receive. In most cases, we're able to very easily show them the differences in the service and still work with them to get them started in a package that meets their needs.

Chapter Twenty-One

Chapter 19: 16 Ways Nonprofits Get Into Legal Trouble & How to Avoid Them

As we wrap things up, we have talked about a number of things that you should and should not do to avoid trouble with the law and with the I.R.S. Here is a summary of a few of the most important things to keep in mind as you are running your 501c3 nonprofit to help you stay out of trouble:

1. Do not forget to file your Form 990 for three years consecutively. If you do, your tax-exempt status may be automatically revoked.

2. Do not lobby or participate in restricted political activity.

3. Do not give loans from the nonprofit to individuals.

4. Do not allow the nonprofit to benefit third parties (e.g., vendors, businesses, etc.) over the general public.

5. Do not allow the nonprofit to benefit insiders in your

organization over the general public.

6. Do not pay yourself or staff an unreasonably excessive salary.

7. Do not avoid paying employment taxes.

8. Do not use nonprofit funds to pay your own personal bills.

9. Do not under-capitalize the nonprofit bank account (Make sure you keep enough money in the nonprofit bank account to pay the bills of the nonprofit).

10. Do not use your tax exemption (or let others use it) for non-charity related purposes.

11. Do not use a name for your nonprofit that you do not own via a registered federal trademark.

12. Do not mishandle funds by failing to use them in the way that you said you would.

13. Do not involve people in your nonprofit that are dishonest.

14. Do not file legal paperwork on behalf of your nonprofit if you do not know what you are doing. Hire a qualified nonprofit attorney.

15. Do not throw away important documents but keep good records (receipts, etc.) to document how funds are being used and how decisions are being made.

16. Do not sign legal documents on behalf of your nonprofit unless you've had an attorney review them.

Chapter Twenty-Two

Final Words from the Author

Congratulations! We have now completed the *"Start A 501c3 Nonprofit That Doesn't Ruin Your Life™"* journey. Hopefully, you now have a better understanding of how to legally structure your nonprofit to avoid I.R.S. trouble, lawsuits, financial scandals & more!

If you enjoyed this book, please consider:

1. Leave a review. This helps the book gain more visibility online to help other people.

2. Follow Us On Social Media - @ChisholmLawFirm and @AudreyKChisholm on LinkedIn, Twitter, Instagram, Facebook and YouTube

3. Buy future books in my Nonprofit Law Series™ (www.AudreyKChisholm.com)

4. Tell a friend (You can also recommend and add the book to your Amazon.com Wish List which helps us reach more people).

5. Visit our website for more information about our nonprofit legal services (www.ChisholmFirm.com)

(www.StartYourTaxExemptNonprofit.com)

6. Sign up for our mailing list here (www.ChisholmFirm.com)

7. Book me to speak on your podcast, at your next conference, seminar, workshop, or event (www.AudreyKChisholm.com)

Chapter Twenty-Three

Special Offer

I have one question for you.

If my law firm could offer you a flat-fee package with no hidden fees to complete and file your application for tax exemption using our proprietary 4-Step Total Nonprofit Formation™ Process would you be interested in a 30-minute free nonprofit consultation? (Value: $450)

Here is what you will receive from the call:

- We will learn about the nonprofit that you want to start
- We will share the next steps to legally form your nonprofit
- We will share our packages and a one-time discounted offer to hire us to form your tax-exempt nonprofit as a bonus for reading this chapter

Schedule your FREE nonprofit consultation today! (Value: $450)

Schedule Online at

www.StartYourTaxExemptNonprofit.com

Or call us toll-free at 1-800-254-6140 to schedule your one-to-one consultation

Chapter Twenty-Four
About the Author

Audrey K. Chisholm is an attorney and the founder of Chisholm Law Firm, PLLC (www.ChisholmFirm.com), a law firm that helps companies and individuals start and grow nonprofits that impact the world.

She started her firm after receiving bad advice regarding her nonprofit from a lawyer that caused her nonprofit to lose its nonprofit status. She fixed her nonprofit and dedicated her life to building a law firm that would help others avoid the mistakes she made early on as a nonprofit founder.

Since then, she has grown her firm into a multi-million dollar company with 20 full-time employees that have successfully handled over 6,500 client matters and 100% of their past clients' nonprofit filings have been approved by the I.R.S. (Disclaimer: Past results do not determine future outcomes.)

Her nonprofit, Revolution Leadership®, Inc., (www.revolutionleadership.org) has served almost 2,000 students and has awarded 40+ college scholarships since 2001.

She is an accomplished businesswoman and a two-time recipient of the Inc. 5000 award that recognizes the top 1% of the fastest-growing private companies nationwide. She is a successful commercial real estate investor and owns apartment complexes throughout the U.S. along with her real estate partners.

She is a SuperLawyer® which recognizes the top 3% of lawyers nationwide. She is a AV-Preeminent Rated Attorney by Martindale-Hubbell® which ranks the top attorneys in the country.

She is a bestselling author of "Start a 501c3 Nonprofit that Doesn't Ruin Your Life: How to Legally Structure Your Nonprofit to Avoid I.R.S. Trouble, Lawsuits, Financial Scandals & More!" which was the #1 bestselling book in the Nonprofit Organizations & Charities category on Amazon.

She is happily married to Dr. Juan P. Chisholm and is the mother of three awesome daughters and one son. She has over 40,000 followers on Instagram.

Follow her @chisholmlawfirm and @audreykchisholm on Instagram, Facebook, Twitter and YouTube.

For more information or booking, please visit:

www.StartYourTaxExemptNonprofit.com

www.ChisholmFirm.com

www.AudreyKChisholm.com

https://www.linkedin.com/in/audreykchisholm

https://www.linkedin.com/company/chisholmlawfirm

https://www.youtube.com/chisholmlawfirm

www.Facebook.com/ChisholmLawFirm

https://www.instagram.com/chisholmlawfirm/

https://www.instagram.com/audreykchisholm/

https://twitter.com/chisholmlawfirm

https://twitter.com/audreykchisholm

www.RevolutionLeadership.org

Chapter Twenty-Five

References & Resources

I.R.S. Tax Exempt and Government Entities

Customer Account Services at (877) 829-5500

www.IRS.gov

Gusto Payroll Service

A company that assists with payroll for nonprofits and businesses. Use my affiliate link below and get a special bonus gift from Gusto:

https://gusto.com/r/miC1p/?utm_source=erother

Chapter Twenty-Six

Special Acknowledgements

My Husband

Dr. Juan P. Chisholm, words cannot describe how much you mean to me and how honored I am to be your wife. You are still the most amazing man I know and I am excited about the rest of our life together!

My Three Daughters

Being your mother is my greatest joy! I am so proud of each of you and as I have told you every night of your life, always know that *"You are intelligent, you are beautiful, you are leaders, you are businesswomen, you are Godly women and you will one day change the world!"*

My Son

Anyone that knows me knows that I love good surprises. Well, you are the best surprise of them all. You've brought such joy to my life and I couldn't imagine my life without you. The world isn't ready for the remarkable things God will do in your life!

Made in the USA
Middletown, DE
05 November 2023

42024754R00116